MUSIC, CULTURE AND CONFLICT IN MALI

by

Andy Morgan

Music, Mausoleums, Ancient Manuscripts, Literature, Film, Theatre and Islamism in Mali

"If music dies, I'll die with it"

Ahmed Ag Kaedi, musician

Freemuse • May 2013

About this publication

Music, Culture and Conflict in Mali
By Andy Morgan

Editor in Chief: Marie Korpe
Production Supervisor: Mik Aidt

Published by Freemuse
Skindergade 15, 2nd floor, DK-1159 Copenhagen, Denmark
freemuse.org

ISBN 978-87-988163-7-9

Second edition

Cover design and photo by Andy Morgan. Front cover of Issouf Eggour, a guitarist of Malian origins living in northern Niger. He is the lead singer and guitar player with the group Alkass.

This book was published with financial support from Svenska PostkodLotteriet and The Roskilde Festival Charity Society.

Table of contents

About the author

Andy Morgan ended a seven-year stint as manager of the Touareg rockers Tinariwen and a 29-year stretch in the music industry in 2010 to concentrate on journalism and writing. During his career in the music business, Andy Morgan worked for a wide range of music companies including Cooking Vinyl, WOMAD, World Circuit, FNAC Musique, Piranha and run his own global electronica label, Apartment 22.

For the past two and half decades, Andy has been contributing music features and reviews to The Guardian, The Observer, The Independent, fRoots, Songlines, NME and Rolling Stone, amongst others. Since 2010 Andy has focused his journalism and writing on the politics and society of West Africa and the Sahara. He has contributed reports about the Touareg and the crisis in northern Mali to The Guardian, The Independent, Al Jazeera, CNN, BBC Focus On Africa and many other publications. He has also given interviews to a long range of tv and radio broadcasters all over the world.

Andy Morgan's next book is about Tinariwen and the story of the Sahara since independence. Andy Morgan maintains a lively website and blog at www.andymorganwrites.com

Acknowledgements and thanks

Although some of this book is based on my own research, parts of it also owe much to the work of other academics, researchers, writers and journalists. I took the decision not to burden myself or the reader by including contextual attributions throughout the book, but I'd like to say a general and heartfelt thank you to those academics, journalists and bloggers as well as the websites and publications that have proved invaluable to me. I'd also urge you get googling and read some of these sources yourself.

Big thanks, in no particular order, to: Adam Nossiter, Adam Thiam, Andrew Lebovich, Assane Koné, Baba Ahmed, Baz Lecocq, Brian J. Peterson, Bruce Hall, Bruce Whitehouse, David Lewis, Gaoussou Diawara, Gregory Mann, Hannah Armstrong, John Hunwick, Judith Scheele, May Ying Welsh, Moussa Bolly, Ousmane Diarra, Patrice Groudin, Peter Tinti, Pierre Boilley, Rose Skelton, and Yvan Guichaoua.

Thanks also to AFP, Africa is a Country, Africa Press, African Arguments, AP, Bamako Hebdo, Bridges From Bamako, El Watan, France 24, Jeune Afrique, Journal du Mali, L'Essor, Le Figaro, Le Monde, Le Republicain, Liberation, Magharebia, Maliactu, Malijet, Reuters, RFI, Sahel Blog, Slate Afrique, The Guardian, The New York Times, and Think Toumast Press.

Thanks also to Assaleck Ag Tita for additional background research. Assaleck is a young and talented Tamashek journalist based in France who is trying to self-fund his passage through journalism school. Any support or opportunities you might be able to offer would be appreciated: assaleckagtita@gmail.com

Thanks to Marie Korpe and her team at Freemuse for commissioning the original report on which this book is based, keeping sane and patient while I turned what was supposed to be a report into a fully fledged book, applying vigorous standards of editing to my work and having the courage to plunge into the 'brave' new world of e-publishing.

Thanks to Mali and the Sahara desert for teaching me to be a better human being.

Andy Morgan, March 2013

1. Destroy the mystery

The Sidi Yahia story

At the end of 14th century, when western Europe was still recovering from the Black Death and the Hundred Years War was only in its third decade, the learned men of the University of Sankoré in Timbuktu bemoaned the distance they had to walk to the great Mosque of Djinguereber, which was then the only major place of worship in town. After a few hours spent teaching or reading treatises on Islamic jurisprudence, philosophy, mathematics, history and geography, plucked from the largest collection of books assembled anywhere in Africa at that time, they found it irksome to step out into the hot dusty streets several times a day, cross the river and brave a long ramble under the Saharan sun.

Someone had a dream in which the Prophet appeared and ordered a new mosque to be built, at a convenient distance just south of the Sankoré *madrassa.* This man, whose name was Sheikh al-Mokhtar Hamalla, answered the summons from on high. The construction of the new mosque dragged on for forty years and even worse, when it was completed, no one wise and respected enough could be found to take charge of the building and become the new imam. But the city fathers trusted that God would eventually send them the right person, so they simply locked the mosque's beautifully ornate front doors and waited.

Not long afterwards, so the legend goes, a man arrived from Walata, a city whose crown of splendour and importance was then in the process of being stolen by Timbuktu. He asked for the keys, opened those great doors, sat down in the cool interior of the mosque and began to hum verses from his Quran. This was the holy man sent by God. His name was Sidi Yahia and he led a rich life full of piety and miracles, revered and respected by his many pupils and followers. After his death, Sidi Yahia was buried in a vault underneath the mosque, which became one of the three great centres of devotion and learning in Timbuktu. Its great doors were closed and the belief arose that if those doors were ever to be opened, it would signal the end of the world. Only judgement, heaven or hell would remain.

Truth? Legend? Superstition? Religious mumbo-jumbo designed to keep the masses of West Africa in the dark ages? Fairy-tales stoked by colonial oppressors to prevent Islamic civilisation from regaining its rightful zenith? There are plenty of scientific materialists in the West who might agree with at least some of those assessments of the Sidi Yahia story. In so doing, they would make very strange philosophical bedfellows with the men who arrived in their 4x4 Land Cruisers with picks and hammers on Monday 2nd July 2012 and proceeded to smash the doors of the Sidi Yahia Mosque into a pile of jagged timber and metal, shouting "*Allah u akbar!* God is Great!"

A group of onlookers stood by aghast. Some were crying. When the sound of splintering wood and ripping metal died down, one of the young vandals, his head covered in regulation khaki cheche, offered 50,000 FCFA, about €80, to the present day imam of the mosque, Alpha Abdoulahi, for repairs. Sidi Yahia's successor refused to take the money, telling the aggressor that it was too late. The damage was all done. "They wanted to show that it wouldn't be the end of the world," one of Abdoulahi's family members told the Agence France-Presse news agency. "They wanted to destroy the mystery," said the imam himself.

2. AQIM, MUJAO, Ansar ud-Dine

The triple headed Islamist occupation of the north

Who are these people who want to destroy the mystery? Who, in the name of Islam, might want to pulverise something so holy and ancient, so cherished by amateurs of Mali's millennial culture and so revered by the people of Timbuktu?

The vandals of the Sidi Yahia mosque were mujahedeen from an Islamist militia called Ansar ud-Dine. They might also have belonged to *Al Qaida in the Islamic Maghreb* (AQIM) or the *Movement for Oneness and Jihad in West Africa* (MUJAO). (In general, I use the more common French acronyms for these various armed groups. The only exception is AQIM rather than the French AQMI.)

The truth is that the lines between the three Islamic armed groups that controlled northern Mali from April 2012 to January 2013 are blurred. They each have their own back story, ethnic mix, leaders and agenda, but there's evidence of considerable coordination and sharing of resources between them. How did they gain control of a slice of desert the size of France and the UK put together? How did an apparently stable African democracy like Mali, which had long practiced a moderate African / Berber form of Islam, become the fief of warlords driven, outwardly at least, by a fundamentalist approach to religion and morality?

Salafism comes from the Arabic word *salaf* meaning 'originator' or 'ancestor'. It describes a belief that Muslims should return to the pure and rigorous moral habits and religious observances of the original followers of the Prophet.

The extremist ideology that ruled northern Mali can be traced back through Osama bin Laden and Ayman al-Zawahiri, the founders of Al Qaida, to Hassan Al Banna, founder of the Muslim Brotherhood, and his fellow Egyptian Sayyid Qutb, the theorist-in-chief of late 20th century Islamic radicalism; through Sayyid Abul Ala Maududi, the father of the Islamic revival in northern India, to an austere ultra-conservative 18th century preacher from Najd in Saudi Arabia called Muhammad Ibn Abd al-Wahhab.

But how did this essentially alien form of Islam, born in Saudi Arabia and bred in Egypt, Pakistan and Afghanistan, take control of a vast slice of the Sahara desert, bringing its population to a state of cowering submission?

On January 17th 2012, a rebellion by the Touareg-led *National Movement for the Liberation of Azawad* (MNLA) broke out in the Malian town of Menaka, which is situated in the far east of the country near its border with Niger. Although dramatic and distressing, this event was neither surprising nor without precedent. The Touareg of northeastern Mali first rebelled against the government in Bamako in 1963 and again, on a much larger scale, in 1990 and 2006. All these rebellions form part of a continual resistance by certain Touareg to central government rule that has lasted for more than half a century. Theirs is a classic nationalist struggle motivated by a desire for political self-determination and the preservation of their unique Berber identity and nomadic culture.

In the last days of March 2012, just when the MNLA seemed to be on the threshold of defeating the Malian army and realising their old dream of an independent state called Azawad, their uprising was hi-jacked by a coalition of armed Islamic groups, in a move whose deft brilliance the 19th century philosopher of war Carl von Clausewitz would no doubt have applauded.

The oldest of these Islamist groups was Al Qaida in the Islamic Maghreb. It was created in 2007 when a recalcitrant Algerian jihadist organisation called *The Salafist Group for Preaching and Combat* (GSPC) decided to align itself with the wider global jihad and become part of the Al Qaida 'franchise'. The GSPC had itself emerged back in 1998 from the most brutal and hard line of all the Algerian Islamist terror groups, the *Armed Islamic Group* (GIA).

The GIA were responsible for the darkest violence of the Algerian civil war of the 1990s. Its acts of terror were so savage and indiscriminate that Osama bin Laden himself expressed concern that its activities were bringing the name of jihad into disrepute. Apart from countless soldiers, policemen and entirely innocent civilians, including women and children, the GIA were also responsible for murdering journalists, writers, intellectuals and musicians, including the star of 'soft' romantic raï music Cheb Hasni, who was gunned down near his home in Oran in 1994.

The GIA's successor AQIM is led by the university-educated Abdelmalik Droukdel aka Abou Wadoud, who runs a jihadist network spanning the whole of the Maghreb and the Sahel from his base in the Kabyle mountains of Algeria. After April 2012, AQIM's Timbuktu branch was under the merciless control of an ex-smuggler from Debdeb in eastern Algeria by the name of Mohammed Ghadir, aka Abdelhamid Abou Zeid, the most feared Islamist *emir* or brigade leader in the southern Sahara. So far, Abou Zeid is the only AQIM emir to have actually carried out a threat to murder a Western kidnap victim when his demands weren't met. Abou Zeid met his end fighting French and Chadian soldiers in the Tegharghar mountains of northeastern Mali in February 2013. Nonetheless, his *katiba* or cell, is still holding 10 European hostages somewhere in the Malian desert.

The second armed Islamist group to control northern Mali was the MUJAO. Led by an ex-jailbird from Mauritania called Hamada Ould Mohamed Kheirou, MUJAO began life in 2011 as a jack-in-the-box terror offshoot of AQIM. Its name popped up first near Tindouf in western Algeria in connection with the kidnapping of three Spanish aid-workers, then a few months later and a few thousand kilometres to the south east in Tamanrasset, where it blew up a police training centre. MUJAO took control of the eastern Malian city of Gao in July 2012, ejecting the nationalist MNLA after fierce gun battles in the city centre. The French army, with some support from the Malian army, finally managed to eject MUJAO from Gao on January 26th 2013. As I write, the jihadists are fighting back with suicide bombers, IEDs and shoot-outs in the streets of the city.

MUJAO is a nebulous alliance of Arab, Moorish and Gao region jihadists, with a strong following amongst the disaffected youth of the Polisario-run refugee camps in western Algeria, the Arabs of the Tilemsi valley north of Gao and Mauritanians angered by their government's pro-Western policies. Some say MUJAO was created after a bitter power struggle at the top of AQIM between Abou Zeid and his arch rival Mokhtar Belmokhtar, one of the most prolific and notorious dons of the Saharan smuggling trade and a senior emir in both the GSPC and AQIM. Having completely fallen out with Abou Zeid, Belmokhtar, so the theory goes, decided to set up his own terror organisation with the help of Ould Kheirou and pursue his own interests independent of AQIM control. Others believe that AQIM itself set up the MUJAO purposefully as a kind of 'foreign legion', whose mission it was to take violent jihad into the whole of West Africa and link up with other jihadist groups already active in the region, such as Boko Haram in Nigeria.

The third Islamist group to take over northern Mali were the lynchpins of the whole affair. Ansar ud-Dine means the 'Defenders' or 'Followers' of the 'Way'. For 'Way' you can also substitute 'Path' or 'Faith'. The group's founder is one of the most remarkable men in modern Saharan history. His name is Iyad Ag Ghaly and he comes from a sub-clan of the Ifoghas, a dominant 'aristocratic' Touareg tribe who have effectively ruled the far northeast of Mali since the 19th century.

Reportedly a brilliant military and political strategist, Ag Ghaly was once the overall leader of the Touareg rebel movement. In June 1990, against desperate odds, he led a small group of poorly-armed Touareg rebels in an uprising against the Malian state and six months later signed a peace accord with the Malian government which secured numerous promises of devolution and development for the northeast. Most of these promises were never honoured.

For a while, Ag Ghaly was seen as a hero of the Touareg cause, their 'Che Guevara'. He was considered by many of his own people to be the only Touareg leader capable of dealing with the complexities of both late 20th century geopolitics and modern desert warfare, and as such, used to be revered and respected by Touareg nationalists throughout the Sahara. Others however suspect him of having sold the Touareg cause down the river by bringing the rebellion of 1990-1 to a premature close, well before the ultimate goal of independence had been achieved. He has a reputation for taking decisions without proper consultation, of being distant, autocratic and too concerned for his own advancement, as well as that of his tribe the Ifoghas, to the detriment of others. His dealings with the Algerian and Malian governments and security establishments are suspected by some to have compromised Touareg interests. In short he enjoys a streaky reputation and has only worsened thanks to his dalliance with AQIM and their violent jihad.

Sometime in the mid to late 1990s, Ag Ghaly came into contact with preachers from the Tablighi Jama'at, a peaceful

Islamic proselytising movement from Pakistan whose *da'wah*, or 'summons', was being heard throughout the southern Sahel at the time. The Tabligh' preached a return to pure and fundamental Islamic principles, untainted either by Western values or deviant local beliefs. Other Touareg leaders and notables fell under the da'wah spell for a while, but few embraced it as whole-heartedly as Ag Ghaly. Between 1998 and 2001, he spent six months at a Tablighi Jama'at centre in Lahore and went on a pilgrimage to Mecca, leaving behind the looser life of women, music and bonhomie that he had been happy to live until then. People close to him relate how he became almost monk-like in his habits and obsessive in the austere simplicity of his devotion. He also forbade his wife to shake hands with men and eventually prevailed upon her to wear a face-covering veil, which was almost unheard of in Touareg female society until then.

In 2003, at the invitation of the Malian government, Ag Ghaly was sent to negotiate the release of 15 European hostages who were being held in northern Mali by a militia belonging to the GSPC. That's when he made contact with the emirs of Algeria's violent jihad for the first time. His work as a chief political fixer and hostage negotiator of choice continued over the ensuing years, bringing him considerable wealth and ever more influence.

In 2006, despite having little to do with its inception, he managed to gain control of a new Touareg uprising and in 2008 he persuaded the Malian President, Amadou Toumani Touré, to send him to Jeddah in Saudi Arabia as a special advisor to the Malian consulate. After eighteen months in the post he was expelled from the country for consorting with 'extremists'. By this time, Ag Ghaly had become an important node in a vast network of power and influence that stretched from Jeddah to Nouakchott, from Tripoli to Niamey and included presidents, ministers, military chiefs, secret service agents, jihadists, tribal leaders, war lords and mafia. In short, he was a man who could not be ignored.

As the Khadafy regime crumbled into dust during the summer and early autumn 2011, Touareg deserters from the Libyan army flooded back into their native Mali, laden with the kind of heavy weaponry that northern Mali had rarely, if ever, seen during fifty years of Touareg revolt. In camps near Kidal, they joined up with local Touareg who had deserted from the Malian army and young Touareg activists who were adept at communicating their message via the Internet to form the National Movement for the Liberation of Azawad. This alliance set about preparing for the rebellion to end all rebellions. However, for ethnic and historical reasons, they made the expensive mistake of trying to sideline Iyad Ag Ghali and exclude him from their project.

In response, he formed his own militia and called it Ansar ud-Dine. Its stated aim wasn't an independent Azawad but rather Shari'a law for the whole of Mali. Ag Ghali then embarked on a rapid recruitment drive, luring young Touareg fighters away from the MNLA with money from his seemingly inexhaustible war chest. Much of it probably came from AQIM, which had become incredibly wealthy thanks to the proceeds of kidnapping and trafficking over the previous five years. Some of it may have come from other sources, possibly from the black ops budgets of Algeria or from wealthy Saudi donors, who were all too keen to see hard line Sunni Islam gain ground in West Africa. Speculation about Ag Ghaly's foreign backers is endless, but hard evidence is almost non-existent.

Money wasn't the only thing that Iyad Ag Ghali and Ansar ud-Dine had to offer the young men of the north east; it was also membership of a well-equipped and well-funded organisation lead by the most admired military brain in modern Touareg history. Although the MNLA's secular, nationalist and Berber outlook was far removed from the

Islamist internationalist and Arabist stance of Ansar ud-Dine, the MNLA leaders felt that they needed Ag Ghaly and his troops in order to defeat the Malian army. So, throughout February and March, the two organisations fought side by side, taking most of the smaller towns in the region by mid-March. This devil's pact was to cost the MNLA dear.

With God on their side

The poorly equipped and badly mismanaged Malian army was sapped of its morale and effectiveness by the military coup that took place in Bamako on March 22nd 2012. A group of soldiers, infuriated by the poor conduct of the war in the north and the sufferings of the average recruit, stormed the presidential palace, ousted President Amadou Toumani Touré and installed a junta headed by Major Amadou Sanogo in its place. On March 31st, Timbuktu, the last bastion of Malian state control in the north, fell into rebel hands. The next day, the MNLA issued a communiqué that declared the independence of Azawad. Mali lost the northern two-thirds of its territory and the country was split in two.

At that crucial moment, Iyad broke ranks with the MNLA and joined his allies in AQIM and MUJAO to swoop down and snatch control of Timbuktu, Gao and Kidal, the three main urban centres in this vast desert region. After a few months of tense and painful coexistence, the MNLA were finally driven out from all three cities by the Islamist triumvirate. In basic terms, MUJAO became the masters of Gao, AQIM of Timbuktu and Ansar ud-Dine of Kidal. Ansar ud-Dine with its 'local' Touareg face, however, became a convenient 'front' organisation for the mainly foreign forces of AQIM and MUJAO throughout the territory. The three organisations divided up the spoils. The Salafist take-over of northern Mali was complete.

The religious 'utopia' that these desert-hardened men then attempted to impose on the people of the north resulted in many atrocities. With God on their side and their black Salafist flags flying high, the mujahedeen foisted their own form of Shari'a law – what you might call 'jungle' Shari'a – on a shocked and frightened population,

Even if you do happen to be in favour of Shari'a law, it is clear that the usual safeguards that ensure that serious punishment is reserved only for the worst crimes, securely proven with due process, were laid to one side in northern Mali. There was also a racist element to the Islamists' application of Shari'a. Almost all the condemned were 'black' Songhoi or Bozo men. Almost all those who judged them were 'white' or lighter skinned Arabs, Touareg or foreigners.

Men found guilty of theft on the flimsiest of evidence had a foot or a hand, or sometimes both, hacked from their bodies. Adulterers or the parents of newborn children born out of wedlock, tried without proper procedure or witnesses, were stoned to death. People caught smoking, drinking alcohol, watching television, playing football, holding hands, walking the streets late at night, wearing jewellery or failing to wear a veil were whipped. All these sentences were carried out in public, in front of grieving men, women and children, often in mass punishments involving many victims. Dancing was forbidden. Gathering with friends was forbidden. Bars and restaurants were forbidden to sell alcohol. The tombs of holy men were destroyed with picks and hammers in broad daylight. Monuments to the martyrs were desecrated. Amulets and talismans were forbidden. People protested and were driven off the streets with sticks, whips and gunfire.

Maybe there was an unexpected truth hidden in the legend of the Sidi Yahia doors. Granted, the world itself didn't end. But perhaps a particular world, all too familiar to people who have visited or lived in Mali, a world of tolerance, community, humorous cohabitation, music, dancing and religious freedom had come to an end.

The deeper causes of the 2012 rebellion in northern Mali and the fall of a once admired African democracy are bafflingly complex and beyond the scope of this report. So are the attempts to rid northern Mali of the last remaining Islamists, who linger in the remote Tegharghar Mountains north of Kidal, in villages around Gao and along the Niger bend up to Timbuktu. It is a struggle that is likely to drag on for month's even years and involve a patchwork of different military entities – French Army, Malian Army, ECOWAS, AU, EU, UN, etc.

The aim of this book is to focus primarily on the effects of the Touareg rebellion, the military coup in the south and the Islamist takeover of the north on the music, musicians and cultural life of the country. This choice does not intend to belittle the general or 'non-cultural' suffering of the people of northern Mali in any way. That suffering has been acute and widely publicised. The focus of this book is culture. Mali is a country whose culture is renowned throughout the world. It is a source of pride, stability and wealth, both human and economic, at home. Culture is Mali's greatest ambassador abroad.

Puritanical doctrinaire Islam is a threat to Malian culture. But unlike some other parts of the Islamic world, where hard line Salafism has drained life and colour from local culture, Mali has proved resistant. It is endowed with deep and well-rooted cultural traditions that the Islamist occupation seems to have been unable to dislodge to any great extent. In some ways, Malian cultural life has emerged with a greater sense of defiance and honed purpose from the experience. Nonetheless, the nation is still in crisis, and its culture still has a battle on its hands.

3. "We don't want Satan's music"

Scenes of musical life under Shari'a law

On Wednesday 22nd August 2012, the following announcement was made by Osama Ould Abdel Kader, a spokesperson for MUJAO based in the city of Gao:

"We, the mujahedeen of Gao, of Timbuktu and Kidal, henceforward forbid the broadcasting of any Western music on all radios in this Islamic territory. This ban takes effect from today, Wednesday. We do not want Satan's music. In its place, there will be Quranic verses. Shari'a demands this. What God commands must be done."

In Gao, a group of teenagers sat around a ghetto blaster listening to Bob Marley. A Landcruiser pick-up loaded with tooled-up Islamic police came by and seeing the reggae fans, stopped and accosted them. "This music is *haram!*" – forbidden by Islamic law – said one of the MUJAO men as he yanked the cassette out of the blaster and crushed it under his feet. "Listen to this instead," he barked, handing the startled reggae fans a tape of Cheikh Abderrahmane Soudais, the highly revered Quranic chanter from Mecca in Saudi Arabia.

In Timbuktu, a young teenager received a call on his mobile phone while he was standing on a street corner in the town centre. As the tinny ringtone sent out a looping riff lifted from a song by local singer Seckou Maiga, it was overheard by a group of Ansar ud-Dine soldiers who were standing nearby. One of them, not much older than the teenager with the phone, broke off from the group and strode over. "Hey! Give me that here!" he ordered. The youth handed over his phone slowly, his face blank and grim. Giving his shoulders an impatient shrug to better seat his AK47, the Ansar ud-Dine fighter opened the back of the phone, picked out the

SIM card, and ground it into the dust with his feet. He then gave the phone back in pieces. "None of that Godless music, understand?!"

In Kidal, a group of women gathered on the dirt airstrip to the east of the town. They sat close, at least thirty of them, in a large huddle of shimmering indigo robes. One woman started to beat the *tindé* drum, while another sprinkled water on its goatskin to keep it taut and resonant. Their chanting ululating rose up to the hazy skies and sent old poetry out to the flat horizons; calling, responding, propelling, forward, me, you, us, all, together. The tindé is the mitochondrial DNA of all Touareg music. Its horizontal trance-beat powers the communal joy of major feasts and gatherings in Touareg lands. Like so much traditional Touareg music, it is played by women and only women. The tindé is an essential ingredient in the glue that binds female society together and gives it power and confidence. But as the men gathered around to watch, as they had been used to doing for as long as they could remember, Ansar ud-Dine militiamen with black headbands and AK47s strapped to their chests sliced into the crowd and shattered it into angry fragments, shouting at the men to keep away from the women and go home. Then they ordered the women to stop what they were doing and go back to their homes as well. The mood burst, and the joy leaked away to be replaced by surliness and frustration.

On the outskirts of Gao, a local *takamba* musician was stopped at a checkpoint on one of the major roads out of town. Takamba is the sound of Gao. With its loping rhythms, sensual dance, skyward vocals and raw cranked-up *teherdents* (lute) and guitars, it has long been the preferred style of musical entertainment at weddings, baptisms and Tabeski feasts in the town and the surrounding country. It is a style that also unifies the Touareg and Songhai people, often at odds with each other, as it is performed and enjoyed by people from both ethnic groups. Gao without takamba would be like Rio without samba; hard to imagine.

Our musician was on his way to a wedding in a village outside Gao, his car laden with instruments and equipment. At the checkpoint he was ordered to step down from his car by a MUJAO militiaman who then proceeded to search it. All the instruments were taken out and piled up by the side of the road; guitars, teherdent, amps, speakers, calabashes. The pile was doused in petrol and set alight. The musician was too scared to shout out, or cry, or flee. There were guns everywhere. He just stood and watched as his livelihood went up in flames. If he made a scene or showed any emotion, he knew that his own life would be in danger.

All these incidents were reported to me either by the people involved or by third parties living in Mali. I have deliberately not used anyone's real name to protect the subjects and their families.

In Timbuktu a posse of local Islamist militiamen turned up at a radio station and took out four large hessian rice bags. They proceeded to fill them up with music cassettes, hundreds and hundreds of them, an entire archive of local musical culture, painstakingly collected over a decade or more. The station manager stood by, distraught, knowing that all this music, that has been a gift to the world and an ember of pride in local hearts, would be lost forever.

In Gao a family watched a programme called 'Mini Star' on television. It is a Malian adaptation of the X-factor idea, in which young up-and-coming singers and musicians imitate the greats of Malian music; Salif Keïta, Ali Farka Touré, Mangala Camara, Sekouba Bambino and others. The performances are judged by a panel and each week a group is eliminated by popular vote. TV is an important means for broadcasting new music in Mali. TV is the family's window onto the world. The weather was hot in Gao and all the windows of the family home were open. A patrol of Islamic policemen heard the sound of music coming from the TV as they passed by the house. They doubled back and entered the premises, grabbing the TV and smashing it out on cracked paving stones of the yard with the butts of their rifles. The family were warned that next time they would get the whip.

In Gao and Timbuktu the dusty streets rang with the synthetic sound of babies laughing, a strangely joyless sound. Forbidden to use musical ringtones on their mobiles, the local population adopted this ironic alternative. The effect was often eerie.

These are just a few snapshots of musical life in what was the most literal and brutal Shari'a jurisdiction in the world.

The MUJAO declaration of August 22nd 2012, was disingenuous for several reasons. First, music had been effectively banned in the north for several months already. The declaration only gave that ban a rubber stamp. Secondly, when the declaration spoke of 'Western' music, Satan's music, it did in fact mean most forms of music; modern, traditional, electrified, acoustic, foreign and local. Only Sheikh Abderrahmane Soudais and his ilk were deemed entirely *halal.*

4. Mosques and maquis

Religion, extremism and law and order in southern Mali

Some outsiders make the mistake of thinking that the hard line Salafi presence in Mali dates back to the beginning of 2012, or to a few years before that. It goes back a lot further. AQIM and its predecessor the GSPC have been hiding out in the northern Malian deserts since at least 2003, kidnapping foreigners, smuggling arms and taking kickbacks and protection money from high-stakes traffickers. But that's not all. A Salafist presence has in fact been growing in the major Malian urban centres, including Bamako, for more than half a century.

The Wahabi strain of ultra-conservative reformist Islam first made its mark on Malian society and religious discourse during the colonial era. It was popular amongst well-educated urban traders, businessmen and students, many of whom had travelled on the *hajj* to Saudi Arabia and brought back the rigorous teachings of Al Wahabi and his acolytes, which, by the mid twentieth century, had become the spiritual cornerstone of the House of Saud and the new kingdom of Saudi Arabia. Some of these fervent hajjis concluded that Mali's religious traditions were in dire need of reform. They saw only obscurantism and backwardness in the old syncretic practices of popular Islam in Mali with its *gri-gris*, talismans, saints and spirits. The way Sufi orders, such as the Tijjaniya and the Qadiriya, were manipulated by the French colonial authorities and subsequently 'tamed' was regrettable, or so these 'progressive' Islamists thought.

Back in the 19th century, at the dawn of the colonial era, it was the Sufi brotherhoods that had presented the most concerted and effective opposition to both animist idolatry and French colonial domination. Now the modernists felt that these same brotherhoods were too pliable in the face of foreign influence, content to promote local 'folkloric' forms of Islam over more 'progressive' Middle Eastern ones. From the 1960s onwards, Saudi petro-dollars were used to promote the Wahabi position by funding mosques and schools in Bamako and other major cities. The traditionalist vs. modernist, Sufi vs. Salafist debate was especially heated when it came to education, with the Wahabiya championing Arabic as the most forward-looking language of instruction, and the Sufi brotherhoods happy to educate their children in a mixture of French and local languages.

But this Wahabi strain was a minor, almost 'cultish' presence in the prevailing landscape of Sufi moderation in Mali. Indeed, the way some Malians talked about the Wahabiya made them sound exactly like a cult, an Islamic equivalent to the Seventh Day Adventists or Jehovah's Witnesses, who went about trying to lure weak and gullible youth into their ranks with all kinds of mind-scrambling inducements. They were considered weird and fanatical by 'normal' people, shunned and even feared. As early as 1957, there were anti-Wahabi riots in Bamako and Sikasso. The Wahabiya were iconoclasts, meddlers, who never tired of telling their fellow Malians that to revere saintly men or allow women and men to mix was utterly sinful. The Wahabi prayed with their arms crossed over their chest, unlike the Malians who followed the Maliki school of law and prayed with their arms hanging by their sides. Wahabi influence grew as they built new schools and mosques. Wahabi-run education was conceived on Western lines, with rigorous enquiry at its core rather than the old Quranic school tradition of just learning by rote dominated in every aspect by religion as opposed to the secularism of the state education system.

Meanwhile the overwhelming majority of Malians continued with their syncretic and comfortably West African forms of

Islamic observance. The Sufi brotherhoods remained central to religious and social life, and as people grew disillusioned with socialism and secular politics, religious organisations became more powerful. A good illustration of this trend is the southern Malian religious movement called Ansar ud-Dine, a Sufi organisation with over a million followers that came into being during the great 'democratic' renaissance of the early 1990s. As the old dictatorial ways were swept away and Mali rediscovered its entrepreneurial flare, thousands of new political, social, educational but also religious organisations came into being.

Ansar ud-Dine south, born in that fervent period of hope, is quite distinct from the armed group of the same name started by Iyad Ag Ghali in the northeast. Its leader is the charismatic Chérif Ousmane Haidara, also known as 'Wulibali' or 'the truth speaker'. His sermons sell by the thousands on video and cassette and his devotees regularly fill the enormous *Stade 26 Mars*, Mali's largest stadium, which is more than any music star can manage today. Haidara's message is essentially one of peace, morality in daily life, clean politics and national renewal, themes that find an easy resonance in the hearts of the many ordinary Malians whose patience with the country's rapacious and self-serving political elite ran out long ago. It is also a message that is delivered in Bamana, the local language. As well as being an inspirational spiritual leader, Haidara is also a patriot who isn't afraid to champion Malian culture and Malian spirituality in the face of those, like the Wahabiya, who claim that Arabic is the only legitimate language for Islamic ritual and discourse.

Some have suspected that links existed between Iyad Ag Ghali's armed Salafist movement in the north and Haidara's peaceful spiritual association in the south. The truth however is that Ag Ghali and the other Al Qaeda affiliates probably chose the name Ansar ud-Dine to try and draw on some of the widespread popularity and trust that the southern movement enjoys. This has more to do with religious 'branding' than anything else. Indeed, after the Islamist takeover in April 2012, Chérif Haidara was quick to condemn the brutality and intolerance of the northern imposters. "Our aim is to raise people's awareness and get them to know that Islam is tolerance. That group they've just created in the north is also called Ansar ud-Dine, but we have nothing to do with them," he told the French magazine Jeune Afrique in April 2012. "Shari'a is for Muslims. Here, in Mali, everybody knows that there are Muslims, Christians, Jews and unbelievers. How can he [Iyad Ag Ghali] bring shari'a and his new Islam to the Malian people? We don't agree with Iyad's shari'a, we reject it."

Hard line Wahabiya dislike the 'cult of personality' that surrounds figures like Chérif Haidara or Mohammédou Ould Cheikh Hamallah Haidara (no immediate relation), also known as The Chérif of Nioro of the Sahel, head of Hamallist Sufi brotherhood. They also distrust the wealth that these hugely popular religious leaders seem to have accumulated. Wahabiya dislike anyone or anything that presumes the position of a conduit to God, or a symbol of God on earth. For them, men can only have a direct relationship with God, without any kind of intercession. But the Wahabiya voice is weak in comparison to the majority. Men like Chérif Haidara and the Chérif of Nioro are not only hugely popular spiritual leaders, they also wield a great deal of political influence. It is said that the Chérif of Nioro often visited the barracks in Kati to talk to coup leader Captain Amadou Sanago in an attempt to temper his excessive and whimsical political machinations.

The High Islamic Council (HCI), led by its vociferous imam Mahmoud Dicko has also gained considerable power in the past two decades. The HCI managed to derail an attempt to reform Mali's repressive Family Code in 2010, ensuring that the laws governing marriage, divorce, women's rights and so on became more conservative and 'Islamic' than they had been before. Meanwhile, more and more women were seen wearing some kind of head covering or veil in the streets. The HCI's power in Malian politics was recently cemented by the appointment of one of its senior leaders, Dr Yacouba Traoré, to the new post of Minister for Religious Affairs and Worship in the government of national unity that was proclaimed in August 2012.

Nonetheless, despite Mali's justified reputation for religious tolerance, the reaction of ordinary Malians to the events of September 11th 2001 differed from that of the average European or American. The murder of 3,000 innocent people was not widely condoned, nor was the stark brutality of the attacks in New York and Washington. But thanks to his bold defiance of the West, Osama Bin Laden became a kind of folk hero in Mali following 9/11, his unsmiling face beaming beatifically from T-shirts, posters and calendars. Of course this didn't mean that all Malians had suddenly become rabid jihadists and Al Qaida sympathisers. Not at all. It just demonstrated a different angle of view on the Islamist struggle, one in which the empowerment of dispossessed Muslims in Africa and Asia and the humiliation of an arrogant Christian West was seen as both positive and inevitable in the long run.

In 2005, following the defeat of Mali by Togo in the preliminaries for the football Cup of African Nations, there were serious attacks on bars and nightclubs in Bamako. The finger was pointed at the HCI and self-appointed Salafi moral vigilantes stoked up by local preachers and mosques, although nothing was ever proved in a court of law. A decree was passed in 2006 forbidding the presence of drinking dens next to places of worship. Between 2000 and 2011, the number of mosques in Bamako tripled, a rate of expansion that exceeded the vertiginous growth of the general population in the city. Often a rich businessman would buy a large plot of land, build himself a fine house and add a mosque or religious centre next to it for good measure. This sacred after-thought ensured that the city authorities would never question or attempt to reverse the development, work on which might have been begun without any agreement from the planning authorities. Meanwhile, the number of bars and shebeens, or *maquis* in the local argot, also grew rapidly.

In 2008, a music venue and *espace culturel* called Le Hogon was closed and a mosque was built in its place. Le Hogon had become world renowned as the place where Toumani Diabaté, the kora virtuoso who is possibly one of the most famous Malian musicians in the world, would perform every Saturday with his group, the Symmetric Orchestra. It was a place of pilgrimage for music fans from all over the world. Following its closure, the newspaper Bamako Hebdo published an article under the title 'Rampant Islamism continues to gain ground in Mali', which claimed that a Malian petrol millionaire by the name of Babou Yara bought Le Hogon with the express intent of giving it as a gift to the descendents of El Hadj Oumar Tall, one of the most famous names in modern West African history.

Tall was a mid 19th century reformer and religious warrior belonging to the Sufi Tijanniya brotherhood who led a jihad through West Africa and established a short-lived Toucouleur empire that covered much of modern day Mali, as well as parts of Senegal and Niger. Bamako Hebdo implied that Babou Yara wanted to please the powerful imams of Bamako by converting a place of fun and entertainment into one of purity and devotion. The leader of the HCI, Mahmoud Dicko, told the paper that in his opinion "transforming an *espace culturel*, a bar or a night club into a mosque is something to be welcomed because those activities sully the earth."

Some musicians and music fans in the capital were shocked by Le Hogon's mutation into a place of worship. The celebrated Malian musician and record producer Cheikh Tidiane Seck told me that the news of Le Hogon's closure was like a knife wound. "Islam in our country has always been moderate," he said. "Now, if we're going to open the door to some kind of Afghanistanisation, or Pakistanisation of our religion, then we're all screwed. The architects of all that must stop calling themselves Malians, because there's never been a more tolerant people than the Malian people. Le Hogon should have been protected. That rich guy could have done what he wanted somewhere else in Bamako, but Le Hogon was symbolic, a place where the music, art and culture of Mali was being developed. 'We must not sacrifice it!' That should've been the attitude of the government at the time."

Toumani Diabaté himself, now a devout and practicing Muslim, refutes the Bamako Hebdo story, claiming that the sale of Le Hogon by the ex-pat Malian family who owned it was just another straightforward real estate deal with no subplot, in a city where real estate was beginning to make fast fortunes. Toumani even tried to buy the place himself but couldn't afford the exorbitant price that was being asked. However, he agrees with Tidiane Seck that the Malian government has never cherished and nurtured the country's cultural wealth as it should. He points out that other 'musical laboratories' where the country's musical culture was incubated, such as The Motel de Bamako and the Buffet de la Gare, have also been allowed to disappear.

The singer Rokia Traore, another global Malian music success story, also regrets the lack of respect and support paid to the music sector by Malian politicians and leaders. "There's this disdain on the part of the government towards the population and I think that artists suffer from the same thing," she says. "Even if the force of things means that we can't be totally ignored and the leaders are obliged to take note of the important role that artists play for Mali, they often say it just for form's sake. They still have to demonstrate that they take artists seriously and aren't treating them as simplistic folk who know how to sing and that's all."

Apart from the story of Le Hogon, which has perhaps more symbolic value than anything else, there has been a tangible seepage of religion into the social life of Mali's urban centres. It is no coincidence that this trend has coincided with an explosion in nightlife; an exponential growth in bars, nightclubs, restaurants, hotels and other places of entertainment, from the swishiest *boîte de nuit* to the most raw and rudimentary *maquis*. Before the crisis of 2012, small clusters of clubs and bars were developing in certain districts of Bamako such as Lafiabougou, ACI 2000, along the Route de Koulikoro and in poorer outlying areas like Yirimadjo and Kalaban Koura. None perhaps deserved the dishonour of being called a fully-fledged red light district but a certain amount of prostitution and drug dealing inevitably attached itself to the wilder and less regulated nite spots. Drunkenness increased, dragging petty violence and disorder in its wake. Some kind of backlash was inevitable. Hedonism and religiosity often dance a kind of dialectical waltz with each other, hand in hand. The *maquis* and the mosque are both protagonists in Bamako's complex social evolution, opposite, but also strangely interdependent.

In an article entitled, 'Journey to the heart of Wahabi Bamako' published by the French magazine Jeune Afrique in October 2011, the ransacking of a small nightclub in the Kalaban Koura district was the starting point for a general assessment of the growing Wahabi influence in the cultural and political life of the city. The article related how a group of people shouting "Allah Akbar! Astaghfir Allah! (God is Great! Seek Forgiveness!)" raided the nightclub of the Hotel Flamboyant in the wee hours of a Tuesday morning and torched the place. When I posted the story on my Facebook page in October 2012, some Bamako residents were moved to comment that these kinds of acts are isolated and that in any case, the level of drunkenness, noise, disturbance and licentiousness in some areas of the city was becoming a major problem. You didn't have to be an extremist to disapprove, just a concerned citizen.

This reaction hints at a wider law and order debate that has been alive in Mali for many years, just as it has in every country in Europe or the world for that matter. How much freedom can individuals possess to break old moral codes and boundaries, to express themselves and to have fun, possibly at the expense of 'decent' society? Are the youth lacking in respect for their parents, their religion and their society in general? Is the government being too lenient in its dealings with drugs, prostitution and petty crime? Are people becoming too lax in their attitudes towards alcohol and dress? Is the country going down the moral drain? All these questions stoke the national debate in Mali as they do in France, Britain or the USA? But in Mali, the debate takes on a religious tint faster than it does in the secular West.

That's not to say that those who proclaim the need for respect, decency, law and order in Mali are all die-hard Wahabiya. Far from it. It is just that these concerns give impetus to a general drift back to core religious values and, in a small minority of cases perhaps, to extreme religious positions. The trend is also helped along by the general disillusionment of the population with the corruption, mendacity and selfishness that has encrusted itself onto the political and social life of the country. Some have even concluded that large religious associations like the HCI or Ansar ud-Dine South are the new de facto political power in Mali. They are the only quasi-political organisations who enjoy the genuine trust and faith of the people.

This concern with law and order and the debate about identity and moral values that accompanies it are nationwide phenomena. In the north, it is clear that noone welcomed the reptilian response to the country's moral dilemmas imposed by AQMI, Ansar ud-Dine and MUJAO. No one should doubt that the application of shari'a law from April 2012 was deeply unpopular in the north and nothing can justify the brutality that accompanied its arrival. It may have been an 'Islamic' solution, although many doubt even that, but it was also alien. It just wasn't Malian.

On the other hand, even in the north, the law and order sub-text cannot be ignored. It seems that one of the main reasons that the MNLA lost their grip on the northern cities after the defeat of the Malian army in April 2012 was that their brief period of control was simply too chaotic, too full of petty pilfering, looting, violence and even rape. Many were moved to say that at least the Islamists imposed some kind of law and order when they took over Gao, Kidal and Timbuktu. The local population might never have expected or wanted shari'a, but it did want an end to the growing insecurity and criminality that had afflicted the region, not only in the previous months of the uprising, but for a number years before that. The irony was of course that this insecurity existed in large part due to the criminal activities of drug lords and trafficking dons with close ties to the Islamist groups.

Mali is experiencing the growth pains of modernisation and this experience is provoking Malians to ask fundamental questions about religion, morality and society, all of which have bearing on the musical and cultural life of the country. Should our life be more governed by religion? Should we be more laissez-faire and secular? Should we resist the influence of Western culture? Should we embrace it? What is our national identity? These topics are hotly debated every day, in the press, in conferences and radio studios, in living rooms and on street corners.

A few years ago, when, on the one hand, Bamako was swinging like it never had done before and on the other, preachers like Haidara and Dicko could draw far greater crowds than any musician or politician, a new style of music rode this return to religion. It was called *zikri* and its leading light was Mahmoud Diaby, whose hit song 'Zoul Koura Nain' topped the ORTM hit parade for several months in 2010. (ORTM, L'Office de Radiodiffusion Télévision du Mali, is Mali's national state-owned broadcasting company). Diaby's sugary melodies and skyward gaze expressed a need for solid truths and divine grace in the midst of struggle and conflict. The music seems to say that the time had come for Malians to reach back to the core of who they are and what they believe in.

Meanwhile, even before the cold shower of rebellion and war that rained down from January 2012 onwards, the problems facing musicians in southern Mali were piling up. Those problems were primarily economic in nature. Piracy, a curse that had been around for decades and which successive governments had effectively ignored, was putting the Malian recording industry into intensive care, if not the morgue. The Internet, but more specifically in Mali's case, mobile phones and their ability to Bluetooth music from one handset to another accelerated this decline. Oussou Bocoum, the boss of a record company in Bamako called Jamnaty Production, told Bamako Hebdo in September 2012 that "in the old days, despite classic piracy, albums could sell around 40 to 50,000 copies. But today, we have trouble shifting 1,000… I have to admit that if nothing is done to protect intellectual property and creativity, record production runs the risk of disappearing altogether."

The sources of income available to musicians were dwindling down to weddings, baptisms or other festive occasions, gigs in hotels, bars and *espaces-culturels*, or tours abroad. In Mali, just as in the rest of the world, DJs, amps and speakers were increasingly taking the place of live musicians, not only in bars and nightclubs, but also at family gatherings and festivities. The cost of hiring a live band, especially an A-list live band or famous singer, was becoming more and more prohibitive.

Even though the dream of performing abroad was still a driving force for many Malian musicians, the chances of launching a successful international career were becoming scarcer for the very same reasons that music in Mali was suffering: the collapse of the international recording industry due to illegal downloading and the lack of money to invest in new artists. Added to those were the costs of putting a Malian band on the road in Europe or America and the increasing difficulty of obtaining visas and work permits.

So life was far from sweet for Mali's musicians before 2012's descent into conflict, chaos and uncertainty, both in the north and the south. However, at least there were still lively music scenes in Bamako, Ségou and Mopti. Up north, the picture had already been grim for years.

The generally accepted notion that Mali is essentially a tolerant country, welcoming, open and mild in its religious faith and habits, is essentially true. Salafism, Wahabism or even just a nameless drift back to stricter more rigorous forms of Islam still play a relatively minor role in the nation's religious life. But they exist and reflect something more general; a gut reaction to globalisation and insecurity, a need for solid moral certainties, a questioning of identity in a changing world and a deep disillusionment with mainstream politics. That does not mean that Mali was craving for the violent jihad that swooped out of the remote deserts and into the towns and villages of the north in early April 2012. That jihad was nurtured in an entirely different mental landscape, one that had been hardened and brutalised by years of guerrilla conflict in Algeria and fuelled by an extreme and pitiless worldview more common to places like Pakistan, Afghanistan, Iraq, Iran, Yemen and Saudi Arabia than Mali. The population of the north craved for security but not religious fanaticism. However, in the end, they had no choice in the matter.

5. Music in the red zone

The Festival in the Desert and the advance of Islamism in the north

"The first time I heard the word *Wahabiya*," remembers Manny Ansar, director of the Festival in the Desert, "was when I was a child in the 1970s. People talked about them as if they were some kind of scary sect. I remember that adults would say to us 'Hey, children, be careful. Those people give children money to lead them astray. Don't take it and don't listen to them.'"

A scary sect. If only it had stayed that way. Before the mid 1990s, political Islam and violent religious extremism hardly blipped the cultural radar of northern Mali. There was conflict in the north of course, but it all related either to the nationalist ambitions of the Touareg, or Kel Tamashek, as they prefer to be known, or to inter-ethnic strife between Touareg and Songhoi, Touareg and Arab or even between certain Touareg tribes clans, often stoked by manipulative politicians and leaders.

If there was a political philosophy that guided Iyad Ag Ghali and the Mouvement Populaire de l'Azawad (MPA) when they fought the great rebellion of 1990 it was a kind of Berber version of Nasserist Arab nationalism, which had been nurtured in Libyan training camps during the 1980s. For the most part, it boiled down a deep desire for autonomy and the right to defend Tamashek culture, the Tamashek language, Tamashek rights and the freedom that the nomad will always carry in his heart. It was a fight for earth, history, family and identity. Islam was part of all these but not the overriding or defining part.

After the Tamanrasset accords of January 6th 1991 that put an end to the rebellion, many Touareg musicians began to 'resurface' and reintegrate into normal civilian life. Members of Tinariwen who had taken part in the fighting found themselves in Bamako or Kidal, playing music, hanging out, doing what they could to earn a living and survive.

Manny Ansar was Tinariwen's manager at the time. He remembers a whole group of Touareg musicians, ex-rebel leaders and *ishumar* who spent time together, in each other's houses, out in the bush or, if they were in Bamako, out along the banks of the Niger, where it was quiet and the nature and solitude reminded them of home.

Ishumar is a Tamashek adaptation of the French word 'chomeur' – the collective noun for the young Touareg men who left their homes in Mali and Niger in the 1970s and 1980s due to drought and lack of opportunity to find work in Algeria, Libya, Burkina Faso and beyond. It was these men who became the foot soldiers of the rebellions of 1990.

Life in the early 1990s was convivial. There was music. Women felt free to come and go. Some people smoked cigarettes and drank alcohol. The bonds between those young Touareg, their music and their culture seemed strong and unbreakable.

No one quite knows why some senior Touareg figures from the northeast, including Iyad Ag Ghali, began to succumb to the message of Pakistani preachers belonging to Tablighi Jama'at. Perhaps it was due to a general disillusion with the nationalist cause, fuelled by the bitter in-fighting and recrimination between different Tamashek tribes and clans that followed the Tamanrasset Accords of 1991 and the National Pact of 1994. Perhaps they were sick of petty politics and yearned for something loftier, purer, and more holy. Perhaps the very notion of dividing up Muslims into nation states seemed suddenly ungodly. The Wahabi have always preached that national boundaries are a Western imposition, designed to divide and weaken the Islamic *umma*, which should by rights exist in one borderless and divinely ruled polity.

"The Pakistani Salafists came through Bamako," Manny remembers. "People saw them with their beards and their white robes. They were nice people. Then they went up to Kidal and that's where certain Touareg leaders came into contact with them." It is hard to establish the precise date when all this happened, perhaps sometime in 1995 or just afterwards.

Manny remembers that everything happened very slowly and gradually. "There was a kind of psychological preparation, done in a really friendly way," he says. "Then certain friends started to distance themselves bit by bit from our circle, people who had liked partying and beautiful women. They were still friends and we would still meet and talk about the situation of the country and the Touareg, but one felt that they were drifting away. They started to disapprove of my lifestyle, the travelling, my friendships with Westerners, the festivals, musicians, alcohol, the life of pleasure. They still had respect, esteem, even friendship towards me but my lifestyle didn't suit them any more. They left very gently."

When they came back from their trips to Pakistan and Mecca, the dedication of these daw'ah devotees deepened. "They were really like monks," Manny remembers, "dressed in white, very simple, eating the minimum, praying all the time, unconcerned about life's problems except spreading messages of peace, togetherness and, of course, God. The first thing that shocked us is that they asked their wives not to shake hands with men any more. Suddenly you would stop seeing their women at all. They would stay in another room where they entertained their women friends."

Meanwhile, Manny had helped to launch the Festival in the Desert in January 2001 at Tin Essako, a tiny little village to the east of Kidal. The festival was born thanks to an immense team effort involving Manny and his EFES association, Tinariwen, the French group Lo'Jo and various other French and Malian funders and supporters. The only threat felt during that first edition was that of petty criminality and banditry. The year before some Dutch tourists had been attacked and murdered up near Tessalit, north of Kidal. On the way up to the festival itself, the truck transporting a small PA system that had been flown in from France was stopped by armed bandits. It took the verbal skill and courage of Kheddou Ag Ossade, one of the core members of Tinariwen who later went on to form the group Terakaft, to dissuade the muggers from taking the equipment and ruining the festival.

A smaller event took place a year later in Tessalit, but it was the third Festival in the Desert in January 2003, and the first in the silky white dunes of Essakane which were to become the festival's permanent home, that really established the event's worldwide reputation. The number of visitors, both local and international, had tripled or even quadrupled. Well-known names like Robert Plant were present. The stage looked like a proper stage. The sound was of the same professional standard as a festival in Europe. The festival had 'arrived'.

And still no sign of any Islamists. A month after that 2003 edition of the festival, the GSPC kidnapped 32 European hostages in the Tassili region of southern Algeria, between Illizi and Djanet. It was the first major crisis involving the kidnapping of Western tourists that the Sahara had ever known. Fifteen of the hostages were sent down into Mali, where they were held prisoner while the chief of the GSPC cell, Amari Saïfi aka Abderrazak El Para, negotiated a ransom with the Malian, Swiss and German governments. A team of northern 'notables', including Iyad Ag Ghali and Ibrahim Ag Bahanga, were sent to speak to El Para and his men. Links were forged and promises were made then that led eventually through many a twist and turn to the Islamist takeover of 2012.

But it wasn't until four years later that The Festival in the Desert began to really feel the Islamist presence in the north. "2007… that's when the red lines were first drawn," Manny remembers, "and the Foreign ministries in Europe and America began to issue all kinds of warnings against travelling to the north of Mali." It was also the year when the GSPC changed its name to Al Qaida in the Islamic Maghreb. Their presence in the Malian Sahara began to be more overt. "The Al Qaida people were wandering around the desert at that time," Manny continues. "But they weren't aggressive. They visited the camps near Essakane and said, 'don't worry, we're Muslims like you.' But then later, their argument began to change. The first alert was when they said, 'we've got nothing against you. We just have the same enemy, which is the West, the non-believers.' That's when I understood that things were going to get difficult, because our festival was based on people coming from all over the world, without distinction."

And then, in 2008 the kidnapping started again with the capture of two Austrian tourists in southern Tunisia. In January 2009, four more tourists were seized on their way back from another music festival called Tamadacht that took place just after the Festival in the Desert in Anderamboukane, a small town up against Mali's eastern frontier with Niger. A Swiss couple and an elderly German woman were eventually freed after many hellish months spent in a makeshift Al Qaida desert camp.

The fourth hostage however wasn't so lucky. Edwin Dyer had lived in Austria for over three decades, but had retained his British passport out of loyalty to the land of his fathers and to the royal family. It was to be his death warrant. The British government flatly refused to negotiate with Al Qaida or pay any kind of ransom. They also rejected Al Qaida's demand to free the Jordanian preacher and jurist Abu Qatada, who was then imprisoned in a British jail. The Al Qaida emir Abou Zeid had Edwin Dyer beheaded on May 31st 2009.

"Things got much worse after the assassination of Edwin Dyer," Manny tells me. "I remember it well. Plenty of people got Tamadacht and the Festival in the Desert mixed up, and thought that Dyer had been to our festival."

"I never received any direct threats from Al Qaida," Manny asserts. "But through third parties, we learnt that some people, Touareg and Arabs who were sympathetic to their way of thinking, were beginning to have an aggressive attitude towards us. 'What you're trying to do is haram,' they told people I knew. 'In the middle of Islamic lands you invite non-believers who come and drink alcohol and commit sins on our dunes.' Once there were even some who came to the Festival site to express their opinion in one of the conferences, or just walk around. But people told me to take no notice. 'They're just trying to make themselves important. Let them talk and they'll go away,' I was told."

Other objectors went up to senior figures in the Kel Antessar, the Touareg tribe that Manny belongs to, and said "Your children are going too far." The Kel Antessar are a revered clan in the Timbuktu / Essakane region, who can trace their lineage back to the Prophet and who have provided the southern Sahara with many of its marabouts and holy men. "Our clan is considered to be the defender of Islam," Manny tells me. "They brought Islam to this part of the world. I remember one of the clan leaders saying to me, 'You know people are complaining about you. They're saying that you're spreading debauchery, that you've created some kind of Sodom and Gomorrah in Essakane. Just be careful. I know what you're doing is beneficial to the Sahara. But take care of our image.' But it was just about morality and good behaviour, not really about jihad or any anti-Western sentiment."

Manny had to increase security measures year by year. More soldiers would encircle the Essakane site, camping out beyond the dunes. And each year, Manny called people he knew in the Touareg rebel movement to ask if it was safe to stage the Festival. They were people with wide connections, who knew the currents and pressure points of Saharan politics. Their answer was always affirmative.

All this was taking place amidst a zeitgeist of fear and antagonism between the West and the Muslim world. The Festival in the Desert was right on the front line. "Everything was connected," Manny says. "The international community, the warnings, Afghanistan, Al Shabab in Somalia, Boko Haram in Nigeria. It was getting worse and worse internationally, and one also felt that the pressure was increasing locally. Al Qaida was getting closer to Essakane. Old friends in Kidal were distancing themselves and becoming radicalised. Mali was getting worried. There was trafficking. Slowly, the screws were tightening."

Then, in the summer of 2009, Manny received a phone call from President Amadou Toumani Toure himself, asking him to move the festival within Timbuktu city limits for safety reasons. The foreign ministry warnings were getting ever more strident. In 2010, Hilary Clinton issued a signed document advising all Americans against travelling to Timbuktu and especially, Manny quotes, "'*not to the world-renowned Festival in the Desert.*' I kept it because it's such a good piece of publicity," he says with a chuckle.

And yet, no one involved with the Festival was kidnapped or murdered. "That was strange," says Manny. "The Festival existed in the same red zone as all the trafficking, and all the other stuff. But they left us alone. I think that Al Qaida didn't want to affront the locals. This festival was considered to be a Touareg festival so to attack it meant attacking the tribes that lived in the area. They knew that the organisers belonged to a much-respected tribe and it was a bad idea to attack their guests. But there was never any kind of agreement between us, never even any word from the Islamists along the lines of 'don't worry, we won't attack you.' There were even those who said that, as we're a family of marabouts, we made prayers and benedictions to block off the road to the festival and keep the Islamists away."

In January 2012, at the last Festival in Desert, Bono asked Manny to call off the soldiers who were protecting him. "I said to the military, 'Look, if he wants to go off like that, just let him do it.' He used to wander off in the dunes; we would take tea there. People think I had some kind of divine force to protect my visitors. And finally, I almost ask myself if it isn't true. Imagine, Bono kidnapped!"

On March 30th 2012, Timbuktu was overtaken by Ansar ud-Dine, AQIM and some units from the MNLA. The takeover effectively evicted The Festival in the Desert from its desert home. At first Manny was very pessimistic, and wondered if it wasn't time to lay the whole enterprise to rest. Then, as musicians from the north started to turn up in Bamako, often with their entire families, begging Manny to find them work, and after talking to his team of co-workers, his friends and his international backers and supporters, he realised that this wasn't the time to give up. Quite the opposite:

"As I'm a pacifist through and through, against all arms and violence, which I wouldn't even use against my greatest enemy, I understood that my only way to resist was to continue to be involved in music, to continue promoting festivals. It was my way of fighting back and showing that you can't kill music just because Timbuktu has been occupied, that Touareg and Malian music will be heard even more and even further afield. If they've closed the doors of Timbuktu we'll open up the rest of the world. We'll go and sing in Tokyo. We'll play *igbayen* – a form of traditional Touareg music from the Timbuktu region – in Rio de Janeiro, we'll sound the tindé drum in Dubai and dance the takamba in Toronto, right up until the day we return to Timbuktu. That's our message. To say that, no, you want us to stop… well, on the contrary. Before our music was heard in Essakane, at the Tamadacht Festival or in Essouk. Today it'll be heard in all the big festivals in the world. So it is the opposite of what you, the Islamists, want. It is our victory and your defeat."

I asked Manny for his reaction to the MUJAO declaration banning music.

"The MUJAO can exist," he answered, "but not among this people. Everything is transmitted in Mali through music, through poetry. So instead of making me panic, at least that declaration told me that we're dealing with people who don't know what they're doing and who won't win. They don't understand the culture that they're operating in and they don't try to understand it either. Mali without music is impossible. Life would have no meaning for the people, because music is their daily reality. It is the only thing that many have, to distract and amuse themselves. They have no television. They have no Internet. They don't play chess. They don't gamble. Music is the only thing that makes life worth living."

6. "Ali Farka would return to his grave"

The end of music in the north

The August 2012 declaration by MUJAO came as little surprise to many musicians from the north. "I didn't even need to hear the announcement," a well-known Touareg musician called Rhissa (not his real name) told me. "I didn't have to find out if music was banned or not. Their presence said it all. That's their identity, so whether they say they're banning music or not, it comes to the same thing: Music is forbidden."

"For the moment there's no music from the north, that's for sure," the guitarist Vieux Farka Touré told me in October 2012. Vieux is the son of late great Ali Farka Touré and native of Niafunké, a sizeable town south west of Timbuktu on the Niger River that was then under control of AQIM / Ansar ud-Dine. "Even just to listen to the radio, or switch on the TV is forbidden. To play music live is even worse."

Afel Bocoum, a singer and guitarist from Niafunké who used to be Ali Farka's oldest and most trusted musical sidekick tried to imagine what the legendary musician would have made of the situation in the town of his birth. "I know that if you were to wake Ali out of his tomb today, he would just go straight back into it," he said whilst the Islamist occupation of Niafunké was still in force. "Knowing his ideas about how to develop Africa, Mali and Niafunké, the place of his birth, I think he would just climb back into his grave, such would be his grief, his disappointment with what's happening today. And I'm sure his life would be in danger if he was alive today, because there was a stubborn man who would want to carry on playing music whatever happened."

"There's a total lack of joy," said another Kidal based musician called Jamal (not his real name) during Islamist rule. "There are no more parties. No one is dancing anymore."

After Ansar ud-Dine took control of the town, Kidal's Radio Tisdas, the Tamashek radio station where Tinariwen recorded their debut album *The Radio Tisdas Sessions* back in December 2000 started to broadcast a stark and unleavened diet of Quranic chanting and Islamic moralising. One can only hope that someone managed to stash the station's unique cassette collection of Touareg guitar music in a safe place.

Tamashek is the language spoken by the Touareg. They refer to themselves as Kel Tamashek or 'the Tamashek speaking people'.

After Ansar ud-Dine was ejected from the town by the MNLA and the French army in January 2013, Radio Tisdas was renamed Radio Azawad. The Maison de Luxembourg, formerly Kidal's premier music venue and *espace culturel*, which was set up and funded by the Duchess of Luxembourg after she fell in love with Touareg music and culture at the first Festival in the Desert in 2001, lay empty and shuttered during Islamist rule. All the hotels, where alcohol was once available and La Grotte, the town's solitary *maquis* or drinking den, also closed down.

Ismaiel 'Massiwa' Ag Ibrahim, who used to organise the annual Camel Fair in the village of Tessalit, about 200km north of Kidal, said that it was impossible to play any music there during the occupation. Until 2009, his small community event welcomed tourists and musicians from as far afield as Britain, France and Arizona. After April 2012 travellers arriving in Tessalit are greeted with a black banner that said, "Please be welcome! Obey Islamic law. It is forbidden to enter with cigarettes. Women must be accompanied by a man to whom they are legitimately related."

"Even traditional music doesn't happen any more," Massiwa continued, when I spoke to him in October 2012. "Perhaps when you're at home, with the doors closed, then you could listen to some music. But if they find you listening to music on your telephone, then it isn't good. I heard of a group of youths who were caught listening to music on their telephones in Aguel'hoc and they were punished but later released."

Tessalit is also the home village of the two of the most famous Touareg musicians in the world. Ibrahim Ag Alhabib, aka Abaraybone, the lead singer of Tinariwen, was born in a nomadic camp not far from the village in 1960 and returned to settle and create a garden by the dried out river bed in the late 1990s, after many years in exile abroad or living in Bamako and Kidal. His fellow band member, Hassan Ag Touhami aka 'The Lion of the Desert', was also born in the region, and moved back to Tessalit in 2007 to build a house made of stone and settle down.

After the rebellion broke out in January 2012, Hassan fled over the border to Algeria with his family and took refuge in Bordj Baji Mokhtar. Ibrahim Ag Alhabib spent most of the occupation out in the bush in the environs of Tessalit. Rumour has it that even Abaraybone, the most famous and revered Touareg musician alive, at times had cause to fear for his safety due to the Islamist presence and spent increasing amounts of time over the border.

For ten months, the north of Mali was not only devoid of music; it was devoid of musicians and, in some places, almost devoid of people. Everyone with the means to travel and take refuge elsewhere fled the country, either to Algeria, Niger or Mauritania, to stay with relatives or to languish in a refugee camp. Others, who were either unwilling or unable to travel so far, left the towns and villages to find safety in the nearby bush, away from the Islamist whip.

On August 10th 2012 the UN Office for the Co-ordination of Humanitarian Affairs estimated that 435,000 had been displaced by the conflict. Following the French intervention and Operation Serval to retake the north, the number is said to have exceeded half a million. It continues to rise every day, especially with the exodus of lighter skinned Arabs and Touaregs from northern towns, fearful of revenge attacks and reprisals by the Malian army. All in all, this has been the largest single migration of people that the southern Sahara has ever known.

When all the village and townspeople went into exile, what was left behind was a vacuum bereft of humanity and joy. Even though there was food in the markets and the rains of 2012 were plentiful, for once, the weeks of gratitude and ease that normally followed the rainy season, when the animals graze on fresh green pasture and the nomads relax and make music, were silent and melancholy for those left behind.

"Almost the whole of Kidal is out in the bush at the moment," Jamal told me in October. "Or in Tamanrasset. Most of the men who've stayed in Kidal have joined Ansar ud-Dine, just to avoid any problems. 90 percent don't have their heart in it at all. But there's nothing else for them. There's just this one lifestyle and you're obliged to follow it. So they pretend to get into the system but they're not really into it. Everybody's under a kind of spell. It's strange."

In towns, music became a clandestine pleasure. "When you're at home you can listen to your music without being hassled, but you can't turn the volume up," Jamal told me. "You have to close your windows and doors and do it very quietly, just to avoid problems."

Some like Ibrahim Ag Ahmed, aka 'Pino', the bassist with the Touareg band Terakaft felt compelled to come all the way to Europe in search of work. "In the north, with the Islamists around, it is impossible to play," he said, back in October 2012. "No one is left in Kidal and those who are still there don't dare say they're a musician. In the south, you can't play because no one would go and listen to Touareg music. It would be like deciding to become a kamikaze if you put on a concert. So most Touareg musicians have left the territory to go to Algeria for example. They do a few small gigs there, in the street, or at weddings and baptisms. With the exception of the well-known bands, all the other Touareg groups have dispersed. It's as if Touareg music hardly exists any more. At times, it looks like it's coming to an end."

Out in the open desert however, far from sedentary towns and villages, the remoteness that has always cushioned Touareg culture and traditions from the world and offered it a form of protection, continued to preserve old liberties. "When I'm out in the bush, at my family's camp, no problem!" Jamal told me. "I turn the volume up full blast. Out in the bush, people can do more or less what they want. You can smoke, play music, relax, no problem."

Manny Ansar corroborated this freedom out in the bush. "I was talking to someone who lives out in a nomad camp near Essakane and I asked him how his life was right now. 'We're living normally,' he said. 'We get together quietly in the evenings and tell poems or sing our songs'. 'But what about the Islamists,' I asked. 'They don't come by,' he answered. 'They go to Timbuktu. We see them driving along the *pistes*, but they don't come to us.' When the Islamists do turn up, out of respect or fear, all the music stops. The inhabitants hide their guitars, their teherdents, their flutes. They hide their charms and amulets. Everything that might upset an Islamist is put to one side, until they've gone on their way, and then it all comes out again. So, you see, it is just a game of hide and seek. There's no acceptance whatsoever."

Listening to music was one thing. Playing was quite another. Ahmed Ag Kaedi, the lead singer and guitarist of the Kidal based Touareg group Amanar already began to feel the sharp edge of the brewing conflict at the end of 2011 when he was reproved by pro-MNLA friends for speaking out in favour of Malian unity and failing to sing poetry about the rebellion. "They took me for a pure Malian Touareg," he told me, chuckling at the memory. "They didn't agree with what I was doing but they didn't do anything to me."

When Ansar ud-Dine began to flex its muscles in the town in March 2012, however, everything changed. The time for talking was over. Whilst Ahmed was away on a trip in Niger, a Landcruiser came to his house and seven Ansar ud-Dine militiamen pitched up to his front door. Four were people he knew well. The other three, including a light skinned Arab who seemed to be in charge, were strangers. Ahmed's sister opened the door to them. "Where's your brother," they demanded to know. "Away," came the answer. "Well when you speak to him next, tell him that if he ever shows his face around here again we'll cut all those fingers he uses to play that guitar clean off." With that, they proceeded to ransack the house and drag all the musical equipment they could find out into the courtyard. Amps, speakers, mics, a drum kit belonging to the Regional Youth office, a mixing desk and several guitars were heaped into a pile which was then doused in petrol and set alight.

When French and Malian troops finally took back Gao, Timbuktu and then Kidal in January 2013, musical life quickly revived. From the fall of Gao on January 26th, to the visit of the French President François Hollande to Timbuktu and Bamako on February 2nd, the citizens of northern Mali rejoiced for a brief period of respite during which the pleasures of dressing up, listening to music, dancing, flirting, smoking were openly indulged again.

Nonetheless, as the President himself said, the road ahead is still long, still fraught with dangers, still completely uncertain. Musicians in Mali have been on the front-line of a war between two different religious philosophies, two divergent conceptions of how to lead a blameless and moral life. It's a clash of opposites that finds its echo in most Muslim countries, although each country sends back its own incarnation of the conflict thanks to the unique set of cultural, social and political realities that prevail within it. It's a clash that often turns musicians, writers, poets, dancers, artists, film directors or actors into cultural combatants, whether they like it or not. But especially musicians because they are, or are perceived to be, the conjurers of love, of sensuality, of joy and abandon, in other words, of all the emotions and states that the Wahabi and Salafi most revile and fear. We in the West call this the war on terror. In Mali itself, and in other parts of the Muslim world more generally, it is more of a war on culture, on a way of life, on freedom. In some sense, it is not a war on terror, but a war on love.

7. "Not like the parties we had at home"

Music in exile

Ahmed ag Kaedi, the Touareg musician from Kidal, told me his terrifying story about Ansar ud-Dine's violence and threats, over the phone from his refugee camp in the Nigerien capital Niamey. He fled there after the Kidal militiamen destroyed his instruments and he performs occasionally for his fellow Touareg in exile. When we spoke, his tone was melancholy and resigned rather than bitter or angry. "Those Ansar ud-Dine foot soldiers in Kidal had nothing before all this," he explained. "Now they've been given money, roles and titles. They use the vacuum that exists up there to feel powerful, to feel like they have a life at last. But they're not doing it for God. I don't think so."

Music doesn't die when it goes into exile, but somehow its energy, joy and confidence diminish. Fadimata Walt Oumar, aka Disco, the magnetic and outspoken leader of the Tartit Ensemble, a group that has done more to educate the world about traditional Touareg music than any other, spent most of the Islamist occupation working in a refugee camp in Ouagadougou in Burkina Faso. "There in the camps life continues," she told me. "When there's a wedding or a baptism, people celebrate with what they have. If there aren't any musicians, they switch on the radio, or put on a cassette by Tinariwen, Tartit or any other band. People dance. Life doesn't stop. But it's not the same life that we had at home. There isn't the same enthusiasm. Women don't make themselves as beautiful as they once did. They're deprived, tired and sad. You go to a party but in truth it isn't really a party, not like the parties we used to have in Timbuktu or Goundam or Gao."

There's also the problem of functioning as a working band in exile. When the members of the Tartit Ensemble were scattered by the conflict that raged around their home near Timbuktu in early 2012, Disco ended up in Ouagadougou, another member of the band made it to Bobo Dioulasso and others went west to refugee camps in Mauritania, thousands of kilometres away. Then the group were invited to play a few concerts in Europe in the summer of 2012 and were inevitably confronted with the problem of obtaining visas, a process that in its own cold and bureaucratic way poses the most basic questions about statehood and national identity.

Were the members of Tartit still Malian nationals? If so, why weren't they travelling to the French consulate in Bamako to submit their visa application as they always had done in the past? Because Bamako isn't safe for Touareg from the north. Well, if Tartit weren't Malian nationals, then what were they? Did they have refugee status? Were they officially recognised as displaced persons by the country that has given them safe harbour? Did France and, more importantly, the French consular officials on the ground in Ouagadougou and Nouakchott recognise Touareg persons from northern Mali as displaced persons with no fixed nationality and therefore deserving of special treatment? Did they bring all their important documents – birth certificate, identity card, previous passports etc – or did they leave them behind in the rush to flee the war? Could their managers or agents in Europe contact them whilst they're in the refugee camp, or staying with friends or family in some remote village?

Disco and other members of the band managed to get their visas in Burkina Faso, with the help of friends of the French embassy. But guitarist Mohammed Issa, who was living at the Mbera refugee camp in Mauritania at the time, wasn't so lucky. The consulate in Nouakchott wouldn't show the understanding or the flexibility necessary to deal with his special status. So in the end he missed the tour.

Similar problems have been afflicting most of the Touareg bands from northern Mali, including Terakaft, Tamikrest and

Tinariwen. The bureaucratic maze that their managers and agents now have to crawl though just to get them to Europe is nightmarish in itself. In this way, important opportunities for Touareg musicians from northern Mali to earn money, support their network of friends and family back home in a time of extreme necessity and speak to the world about their plights and their dreams, are lost in flows of paper and procedure.

8. Bamako – a musical Mecca in crisis

Political and economic meltdown in Mali's capital city

The rebellion, the military coup and the Islamist takeover in the north delivered a flurry of blows to the music scene in Bamako, which had already been shoved on the ropes by piracy, the internet, recession and the trend of replacing live music with DJs. The precise toll of the decline in musical activity since March 2012 varies depending on who you talk to.

"Life for musicians in Mali is very difficult at the moment," Amadou Bagayoko, one half of Amadou & Mariam and President of FEDAMA (the Federation of Malian Artists) declared in October 2012. "Musicians used to play in night clubs and *espaces culturels* but as people aren't coming to Mali anymore to listen to music, it means that hotels, bars, restaurants are working less well and so musicians can't earn a real living any more. If it was 80 percent capacity before, I would say it's about 40 per cent now."

"Musical activity has diminished by 98 per cent... NINETY EIGHT PER CENT!" was Toumani Diabaté's emphatic lament. "I was the leading musician here in Bamako who continued to play in the small *espaces culturels*. Because even when activity was at 100 percent, it wasn't everybody who agreed to play in those places. But I chose to play live every weekend with my band. It gave people an opportunity to hear live music here in Bamako. After March 26th 1991, when democracy arrived in Mali, many nightclubs stopped hiring bands and so we started to play in *espaces culturels* instead."

"It was only there that you could hear live music, because the nightclubs were just playing CDs and cassettes. But today the truth is that music has gone; entertainment has gone. The coup d'état happened months ago, but we haven't performed since, because people don't have the head for having fun at the moment. They don't have the money. They're suffering. There were all those problems between the Red Berets and the Green Berets, which means there's a lack of security. So if you don't have the money and you feel insecure, you're not going to leave home, are you. We musicians have been dealt a big blow by all of that. A big blow!"

Red Berets and the Green Berets were different fractions in the Malian army who were in conflict after the military coup.

The world-renowned bandleader and ngoni player Bassekou Kouyaté told me that Le Diplomate, the *espace culturel* to which Toumani Diabaté and his Symmetric Orchestra moved their regular weekend residency after the demise of Le Hogon, had also closed its doors. "And there's L'Hotel Amitié," Bassekou continued, "350 people have been made redundant there. All the large hotels are suffering. No tourists are coming to stay, or very few anyway. We put on little events, but there aren't many places to play now. They've closed because of the crisis. People don't have a lot of money. There isn't much of a clientele who go out at night. What people earn they use to feed themselves, not to have fun."

Adam Thiam, one of Mali's leading journalists and a regular contributor to Le Republicain and other papers, also said that musical life dropped markedly in intensity after the coup, although not to the statistical extent claimed by Toumani Diabaté. "Our big artists have tried to maintain their usual commitments as much as possible," he told me. "Oumou Sangaré is still playing at her hotel, the Wassoulou. Balla Tounkara is still a regular fixture at the Espace Kora and Salif Keïta has started a residency at the Mouffou for his fans. But these places are less and less full. People don't go out much, because of all the security issues, even if it must be said that Bamako, despite the current problems, still seems to be a safer city than Nairobi or Abidjan. But people aren't used to meeting soldiers in the streets, so they tend to stay at home."

"The life of musicians in Mali is like the life of the population in general," said Cheikh Tidiane Seck, "in reality we're all being held hostage. Going out to unwind and listen to music… well, people aren't necessarily in the mood for doing that anymore."

This slump in joie de vivre was a catastrophe for musicians. Music is to a city what mosses and lichen are to a forest; a sign of vitality, resilience and a strong, healthy eco-system. A music scene thrives when a country prospers and when people feel relatively safe and optimistic. Conversely, when a country is laid low by social and economic crises, music and entertainment suffer. Musical life is the barometer of social well being.

"The truth is that in Mali," says Rokia Traore, "artists that don't have an international career find it hard to live properly, and by properly I mean enjoy a good career and a decent retirement. You can easily understand that what is difficult for a European musician is just hell for an African musician at the best of times. Life was already precarious even before the crisis. So it is not too hard to imagine the situation of those musicians in a time of war."

Rokia's own NGO, La Passerelle, has had to cut its projects by half and send far fewer artists out on the road. The organisation is still pursuing an ambitious project to build a concert hall in Bamako, but the pace of work has slowed, even though Rokia and her team are making every possible effort to continue paying its workmen.

Most of the people I interviewed knew cases of fellow musicians falling below the breadline and being forced to beg for money, or selling their instruments for a song, just to eat and buy a few essentials for their children's schooling. "It is dramatic," Rokia Traore says, "the number of artists who came along and who hadn't eaten for three days, who had kids who go to school and who hadn't been able to buy what they need, who were ill and hadn't been able to get treatment. It's just a catastrophe."

During the Islamist occupation of the north, a huge influx of northern refugees, with musicians inevitably amongst them, piled extra pressure on Bamako's existing problems. "All the musicians have left the north," Vieux Farka Touré lamented back in October. "They're all in Bamako, Mopti, or elsewhere. There's no point staying if they can't play. There are weddings in Bamako, or baptisms, and a bit of work in bars. But it is only if you're lucky enough to know people."

"Musical life has stopped in Bamako," said Afel Bocoum. "Everybody is scared of going to Mali now and it's the tourists who make musicians play. Hotels give us our livelihood. But none of that exists anymore. On top of that crisis there's another crisis. Every Bamakois has a relative in the north, and now they have the job of feeding those relatives. They don't even know where they're going to find the money to look after them."

In times of loss and distress, it's not only the ability to perform that suffers but also the urge to write new songs that can weaken and disappear. "My job is playing music, but with all these problems, you don't even have the inspiration to write new songs," Afel Bocoum told me during the deepest days of the crisis last September. "You don't even feel like touching your guitar. You're just thinking about home all the time. My father lives there. My mother lives there. And you hear that they're raping young people. If they aren't yours then they're your neighbour's. The heart is wounded."

However, even in the depth of the crisis, there seemed to be three essential struts of the local music scene in Bamako that continued to exist in a relatively healthy way, although they didn't exactly thrive in comparison to former times. One was the traditional djembe-driven street dancing sessions, known as the *sounou.* "It is when women pool their money and invite a couple of musicians down to have some fun," Adam Thiam explained. "Those are carrying on. They aren't events that are promoted in advance or anything and they haven't really been affected by the crisis. But their frequency has diminished."

"The sounou are still happening," agreed Violet Diallo, former British Consul and long-time resident of Bamako. "You hear them. It's quite funny, the other day I heard some noise going on in a street I was driving towards and I thought, "that's nice, it is a sounou." But when I got there it was some kind of Islamic preaching outfit. You don't quite know what you're getting into."

The other solid bedrock of musical life in Bamako were the weddings, baptisms and other festive family occasions. Sundays continued to chime to the klaxons of wedding corteges as they made their raucous way through the streets, holding up the traffic at the main downtown intersections.

"There are fewer big weddings happening than there were before," Violet explained. "One thing is that they're expensive. A big name like Babani Koné will set you back two or three million FCFA (€3,000 – €4,500). And there aren't that many people with that kind of money to fling about any more. So most musicians are turning their eyes abroad for salvation. I've had several coming to ask for help to fill out visa applications to the US or Europe."

"Weddings are still happening, every Sunday," Bassekou Kouyaté told me. "But now even weddings are beginning to cut back on the live music. People just buy a CD player, bring some loudspeakers, and dance to the CDs instead. They play the music by artists they would love to invite but don't have the means to do so."

"It is the rappers who are still playing everywhere," said Toumani Diabaté. "And a few griottes who sing at weddings. Despite all the problems people are still getting married. And baptisms continue to happen because babies are still being born. So that keeps a few griottes employed, but even with that there are many, many difficulties."

Lastly, there were the nightclubs and bars, the places that ditched expensive live shows some time ago and now survive on CD turntables and pumping speakers. "People still go to the clubs, that's for sure," said Vieux Farka Touré, "Many people frequent Le Savannah, or the Parc des Princes, or the Domino and places like that. Every Saturday, there's stuff happening there. There are plenty of musicians who try to take advantage by going to those places and playing a bit, earning a crust. But it is not really a living."

Many an eyewitness report of the Bamako mood during the crisis of 2012 remarked on the resilience of daily life in the capital and how it refused to succumb to panic and fear. In an article entitled 'In Bamako, the war is far way', Slate Afrique claimed that "whoever chooses to tour around Bamako by night will find it hard to believe that this is a country that's supposedly cowed by current events and whose fate is being discussed by the United Nations. The partygoers haven't changed their habits and the bars, restaurants and nightclubs are still open for business."

However, the article also went on to admit that any business dependent on tourism was suffering. Furthermore, if you believe the gloomy assessments that emerged from the mouths of musicians, it seems clear that whilst Bamako club life might be resilient, even defiant, it no longer provides local musicians with a livelihood. Like everywhere else in the world now, music appears to survive without musicians.

There were still some voices of optimism in Bamako in September 2012. "The period we've been through isn't the tourist season," said Lucien Roux, director of the French Cultural Centre in Bamako. "There were tourists who used to go to Le Diplomate to listen to Toumani Diabaté, but they were never the main bulk of the clientele of cultural and artistic life in Bamako. I've been told… because I don't go much myself… that the nightclubs are full every weekend. The youth are keener to party, without a doubt, perhaps to relax and take their mind off all the problems for a while. On the other hand, for the traditional artisans and jewellery sellers, the lack of tourists is of course a serious problem."

9. Get up stand up!

Malian musicians protest and survive

During the long months of the Islamist occupation, when Mali was divided into two battered halves, Malian music was on the ropes but it was never defeated. In fact, if anything, the crisis brought out a fighting spirit among Malian musicians. It galvanized certain sectors of Mali's creative community into a mood of uncharacteristically active defiance, musicians among them. A certain mild contentedness, an easy faith in melody, good grooves and providence, which had always guided Malian music in its essential conviviality and gentleness, gave way to more urgent passions.

On May 23rd 2012, a press conference was held at Mouffou, Salif Keïta's *espace culturel*, to announce two major events to raise funds for humanitarian disaster relief in the north. The first was a telethon and VIP soirée organised by the Malian Red Cross and Salif Keïta's UAAPREM (Malian Union of Artist, Producer and Music Publisher Associations), which took place at Bamako's International Conference Centre on June 21st. Many headlining Malian names were there including Bako Dagnon, Nayini Diabaté, Vieux Farka Touré, Oumou Dédé Damba, Babani Koné, Khaïra Arby, Baba Salah and Salif Keïta. The interim Prime Minister, Cheikh Modibo Diarra was also in attendance. Entrance to the VIP gala was 20,000 FCFA, about 30 Euro, a fortune in local terms. Members of the public also donated in their thousands over the phone and the Internet. 36.6 million FCFA (c. 56,000 Euros) was raised before the curtain came down at one o'clock the next morning.

The second event was a huge concert that took place in the Modibo Keïta Stadium on June 28th. From 6pm in the evening until 6am the next morning, a carnival of Malian rappers and play back artists paraded on stage, with all proceeds going to help the people of the north. Salif Keïta and Oumou Sangaré were otherwise engaged and could not attend. Zongo, a famous comedian who is half Ivorian and half Burkinabé, took the stage to the great delight of the crowd. The singers Bako Dagnon and Tata Bamba Kouyaté were hailed with the biggest cheers.

Bako Dagnon took the opportunity to urge Mali's soldiers to show their courage and take the fight to the Islamists in the north. "When you're courageous, nobody dares defy you," she said. "Mali is a courageous country. No person dared to defy Mali before. I pray to God that they [the soldiers] are not fearful and that they liberate Mali!" Proceeds from the concert were donated to the Malian Red Cross for the relief of the distressed population in the north.

On the 22nd September 2012, the 52nd anniversary of Malian independence, Cheick Tidiane Seck organised a 'Gathering for Peace in Mali' at the *Palais des Congrès* in Montreuil, the eastern suburb of Paris that is home to the largest population of Malians outside Mali itself. Manu Dibango, Oumou Sangaré, Baba Salah, Amadou & Mariam, Lokua Kanza, Vieux Farka Touré, Oxmo Puccino, Fantani Touré, Jean-Philippe Rykiel and over thirty more artists came to perform and plead for peace and reconciliation. "It was a moment of communion," Cheikh Tidiane said, "We got together on the anniversary of Malian independence to denounce what's happening out there, without any disavowal of the politics involved. Because, well, you need a bit of everything to make a world. But the opinions of this or that person aren't important to me. What's important is the rediscovery of our country that my ancestors took time to create, back in the time of Sundjata Keita. Because there was never a more peaceful country than Mali."

"No Malian artist can sing right now without singing about what's happening," the journalist Adam Thiam told me back in October 2012. "Artists are reacting to the crisis. Those reactions can be inclusive like Oumou Sangaré, who has done a song called 'La Paix' ('Peace') for her forthcoming album. Or they can be aggressive, like some of the younger generation who accuse the Touareg of being at the root of all that is happening to Mali."

The promisingly titled *Association for Changing Behaviour* brought together 18 girls and boys aged from 8 to 12 years old from all over the country, representing all the major ethnic groups, to perform a song entitled 'A Call to the Leaders of Mali'. It was sung in eight different national languages – Arab, Bambara, Dogon, Peul, Senoufo, Soninké, Songhai and Tamashek – by the children, most of whom were the sons and daughters of griots and many of whom had already proven their worth on the hit Malian TV show *Mini Star*, in which young up-and-coming singers and musicians imitate the 'greats' of Malian song. The Bambara passage of the song went *"We may be hungry, thirsty, poor, but we have our dignity. But if there is no peace, we risk losing that dignity. We invite all the ethnic groups to reach out their hands and develop Mali."* The chorus went *"Mali will never be divided."*

The arrangement of the song mirrored Mali's ethno-musical variety and included passages of Malinké *mandan*, Bambara *bara*, Songhai and Tamashek *takamba*. All the children were clothed in the various traditional garbs of their ethnic group. The idea for this rainbow band of Malian youth came to Adama Diarra, the president of the Malian Red Cross, while he was leading a mission to Timbuktu to create a humanitarian corridor in the north. He was especially struck by the suffering of children embroiled in the conflict, and felt that their voices weren't being heard. On 22nd September, Independence Day, the group performed at the French Institute in Bamako and later they played in front of the interim President Dioncounda Traoré. An album is being planned with all proceeds going to help children affected by the war.

This kind of expression of national unity through music has a long pedigree in Mali. In the early years of independence, both President Modibo Keïta and his successor Moussa Traoré attempted to bind their young and scattered nation together using the *Semaines de la Jeunesse* ('Youth Weeks') and Cultural Biennales, in which music, dance and theatre troupes from all over the country would travel to different regions to perform, compete and rub shoulders with their counterparts in other ethnic groups. In the hands of the country's politicians and leaders, music became a tool to change social attitudes and create pride in a single nation with many different rhythms, languages and cultures.

Whereas in other socialist countries, quasi-militaristic youth organisations like the Young Pioneers were used to create nations with a common sense of identity, in Mali this process was engaged through music. Even though recurrent waves of Touareg separatism show that the policy was never entirely successful, the relatively peaceful co-existence of Mali's other cultures proves that it wasn't a failure either, far from it.

The Festival on the Niger in Ségou, one of the most successful and stable of Mali's large annual music festivals, has also been reacting to the crisis with inspiring courage and dedication. In an interview for Voice of America radio, the festival's founder and director Mamou Daffé told the anthropologist and writer Heather Maxwell that Ségou had become Mali's "zone of confidence; its artistic and creative zone."

The Festival on the Niger Foundation and the Kôré Cultural Centre which it runs, have been staging regular events in the town since the military coup in March 2012, attracting not only most of Mali's well known musicians, but artists from other creative disciplines including visual art, dance, puppetry, multimedia and traditional crafts. "Ségou is profiting from the situation to strengthen its reputation as the cultural capital of West Africa," Daffé told Heather Maxwell.

The theme of the 9th edition of the Festival, which was due to be held in February 2013, was to be Timbuktu. This was partly in reaction to the MUJAO's declaration banning all secular music in the north but also a way of warmly welcoming the homeless Festival in the Desert, which was to be invited as an honoured guest. In mid-January, as the French air force was bombing Islamist positions all over the north, and French ground forces were battling an AQIM counter attack in the town of Diabaly, up towards the Mauritanian border, Mamou Daffé was still holding out hope that the Festival would take place. But on January 23rd 2013, he issued a press release declaring that, given "the barbaric aggression from terrorists, drug traffickers and separatists", it would be impossible for the Festival to go ahead.

The news was sadly inevitable. The Islamists had advanced as far as Konna, a town on the main tarmac road between Mopti and Douentza. Ségou was only 3oo miles further down the same road. Daffé and his team had shown admirable courage and mighty perseverance in the months leading up to the Islamist attack, but there had to be a limit. Musicians may be on the frontline of the cultural war, but the war of RPGs, AK47s and helicopter gunships is best left to the soldiers.

A few days later, on January 25th, the Festival in the Desert also announced that it was postponing it 13th edition, which had been due to take place at the end of February 2013 near Ouagadougou in Burkina Faso. It also announced the postponement of the two Caravans of Peace, one of which had been due to travel down from the refugee camps in Mauritania to Bamako, then East to Ségou and finally on to Ouagadougou, and the other from Tamanrasset in Algeria, down through Niamey, the capital of Niger, and finally to Ouagadougou where it was going to rendezvous with the first Caravan in a great desert carnival of music and defiance. It was not to be.

"As you are likely aware," the press release started, "Mali has entered a State of Emergency. This week, the government has requested that we temporarily postpone the Sahel portion of the Festival, as insecurity in the region could jeopardise the safety of tourists, technicians, artists, journalists etc. The February caravan in the Sahel will be postponed most likely until late fall, after the rainy season." The communiqué then went on to speak about the Festival-in-Exile, which, so the plan goes, will have a global as well as a Sahelian dimension.

The cancellation of two of the highest profile musical events in Mali's cultural calendar should not be taken either as a sign of timidity in the face of the Islamist assault on culture and music or one of surrender. The spirit in which the teams behind both Festivals battled against the odds to try and keep their events on track was bold and redoubtable. Both kept the hopes of musicians and fans alive for as long as possible. Both rose to a challenge that had mutated into something epic and essential and embraced the fact that they were now part of a struggle with far greater resonance than mere musical notes; a struggle between the cold dream of religious utopia and impossible perfection on the one hand, and a simple faith in humanity on the other, a faith which gives men and women the space in which to indulge their senses and search for a beauty that reflects the divine, even if it also gives them space to err and be human.

That same spirit of defiance motivated other initiatives both great and small. The great afro-reggae star Tiken Jah Fakoly, himself no stranger to persecution and war, both of which have ravaged his native Ivory Coast, recorded a special song called *'An Ka Wili'*, which means "Mobilisation and

Galvanisation" in Bambara. It was released just after New Year's Day 2013 and given away for free in Mali.

"I've released this single to support Mali in its time of need," he told Jeune Afrique. "The single is a call for general mobilisation. Mali has known great men, great empires and it's unimaginable to allow the country to be cut in two as it is today. Malians must count first and foremost on their own forces."

The musical statement that dominated the headlines throughout January and early February 2013, achieving the widest global reach of all the Mali crisis initiatives, was *'Mali-ko'* (Peace), a song recorded at the famous Bogolan studios in Bamako by Mali music's roll of honour: Toumani Diabaté, Khaïra Arby, Tiken Jah Fakoly, Baba Salah, Habib Koité, Bassekou Kouyaté, Oumou Sangaré, Amkoullel, Vieux Farka Touré, Amadou & Mariam, Kasse Mady Diabaté, Afel Bocoum, Doussou Bakayoko, Sadio Sidibé, M'baou Toukara, Fati Kouyaté, Soumalia Kanouté, Master Soumi, Iba One, Mylmo, Djelimady Tounkara and last but indubitably foremost in this hugely successful endeavour, Fatoumata Diawara.

Fatou, as she's known to many Malians and a swelling number of fans throughout the world, is a young singer, songwriter and actress who only really began to make a dent on the global consciousness in the first half of 2011. In many ways, she could be a poster-girl for a Malian generation that is coming into its own just as their country faces the blackest moment in its short history as an independent nation. She is beautiful, smart and extremely talented. But 'Mali-ko' also revealed the fighter, motivator, federator and organiser in Fatou. For several months after its release in January 2013, Fatou was a permanent fixture on the global airwaves, giving interviews, performing the song, explaining the background and teaching the world about Mali.

Every tragedy has its silver lining. Mali's battle against the bearded joy killers has focused the attention of the world on its miseries, its complexities and its music like never before. It took the French intervention and Mokhtar Belmokhtar's assault on the gas works at In Amenas in Algeria for the West to reach a state of full alertness about what was happening in the Sahara and the Sahel, but when it did, the effect was immense. Mali, that dusty forgotten ex-French colony, which had never once hit the headlines in Britain or the USA in the fifty years of existence on the margins of the world's consciousness, was suddenly at the top of every political to-do list and media agenda from Washington to Tokyo and all points in between.

Energised by Mali's agony, Malian musicians have ridden the wave with grace and resolve, none more so than Fatou. She has appeared on the kind of prime-time TV news and chat shows that would never have considered inviting her before the world woke up to the Malian tragedy. Not because she's unworthy of such exposure, but simply because mainstream TV producers had such a narrow concept of what might inspire and intrigue their audiences. The result is that awareness of Mali's deep and rich musical culture has surged exponentially, far beyond the faithful realm of the world music fan. Whether the effects of that surge will last, no one can tell. But in amongst the fear, the anger, the frustration and desperation, Mali needs a few positive news stories and music has been providing them.

In some respects, music, seemingly so battered and abused during Mali's darkest hour, has done the country a great service. Without that immense musical wealth, the global reaction to Mali's crisis would no doubt have been equally sympathetic and widespread but possibly not as enchanted and empathetic as it has been. Somalia also has a rich and ancient tradition of music and poetry but because its worldwide musical output has never been as prolific as

Mali's, the Somalian civil war has been a tragedy without a soundtrack, without poetry to distil the national agony, with a few notable exceptions of course. News editors, for all their faults, are often delighted and immensely relieved to have a musician on their show to explain the crisis in some distant country, rather than a politician, a general, a security expert or a professor of international relations. It adds an accessible and attractive touch to the coverage. That huge reserve of music, which successive Malian politicians have been content to patronise and generally ignore, has proved once again to be the country's primary asset, its saving grace.

Could Mali's musicians and musical activists have done more? No doubt. But their reaction to the worst crisis in the history of their nation has been unusual in many ways. Malian music has never been a stranger to politics or social commentary, but its unwritten rules of engagement have generally been pacific and disarming. Head on confrontation was often softened or even avoided with lyrics that were full of metaphor and allusion. Collective action, with many artists coming together as one to raise a single united voice on some pressing issue has never been a prominent part of Mali's musical story. A sense of brotherhood and sisterhood amongst Malian musicians and artists has always existed, but the need to proclaim it and unfurl it as a rallying flag has rarely been felt. Telethons, benefit concerts, songs, multi-ethnic choirs, they all demonstrate that Mali's musicians are capable of fighting back, especially when their art and their livelihoods are under direct threat.

In terms of plain talking, however, of bare-knuckled protest rhyming, none of the initiatives outlined above have come even close to what the Malian rappers have been conjuring up since the crisis began.

10. When the going gets tough, the rappers get going

Mali's Facebook generation steps up

Malians have no trouble finding role-models in their own history to help them feel proud of who they are: Sundjata Keita, Mansa Musa, Sunni Ali, Mohammed Askia, El Hadj Oumar Tall, Cerno Bokar, Samory Touré. The last name in that list was a thorn in the side of the French army for more than two decades at the end of the nineteenth century. He's also the subject of many Malian songs that laud his strength, wisdom, bravery and endurance. During the long months of Islamist occupation of the northern two-thirds of their country, many Malians were asking where those qualities had disappeared to, just when they're needed most.

Samory Touré's warriors were called *sofas*. Hence the name of one of the most radical and outspoken musical organisations to have sprung up in reaction to Mali's current tragedy; Les Sofas de La Republique. The group – Les Sofas aren't your classic 'band' as such, think of them more as a rap posse, a self-help association, a pressure group, a political party, an educational charity and a think tank, all rolled into one – came together in Bamako's Badalabougou district the day after Captain Sanogo's military coup on March 22nd 2012. At its core were the rappers Ramses aka Sidi Soumaoro, son of the famous Idrissa Soumaoro, Dixon and Djodama from Tatapound, the band that revolutionised Malian rap in the 1990s. Joining this trio were a small tribe of musicians, bloggers, web designers and other activists and 'hacktivisits'.

Les Sofas de la République released two songs; 'Ça Suffit!' ('That's Enough!') and 'Aw Yé to An Ga Lafia' ('Leave Us In Peace!'). Both of them fired off an impassioned plea, not only to Mali's political and military leaders, but also to the Malian people, who, in the eyes of Les Sofas, were guilty of sleep-walking into the crisis thanks to their passivity, their cynical acceptance of corruption and their willingness to let the country's precious democratic system putrefy and go bad. At the heart of Les Sofas' message was an invitation to the nation to look deep into itself and examine the root causes of their present fall from grace, with intelligence, honesty and courage.

On the video of 'Ça Suffit', Les Sofas start by expressing their respect for all the soldiers fallen on the field of battle, and their solidarity with the people of the north suffering from aggression. Later in the song, Dixon raps out the line *"Coup d'États in Africa, corrupt soldiers, opportunistic politicians – THAT'S ENOUGH! Demagogic politics, populist and corrupt, inactive citizens – THAT'S ENOUGH!"*

'Aw Yé to An Ga Lafia' was released following the extraordinary attack on the interim President Dioncounda Traore in Mali's 'White House', the Kọulouba Palace in Bamako, by a mob of protestors stirred up by Sanogo and opposition parties on May 21st 2012. This attack seemed to sully all that remained sacred in Mali's troubled democracy and shocked public opinion to the core. "*Malians against Malians, fiercer and fiercer yeaah,*" rap Les Sofas, "*Taking up arms and making blood flow yeaah. Making tears flow and making us lose time, bothering us with stupid details… Our relatives are dying up in the north while we try and agree on who will take the tiller.*"

Both of these songs as well as the video of 'Ça Suffit' were banned by Mali's state broadcaster ORTM, who deemed that the moment wasn't propitious for inflammatory rap tunes. Both nonetheless became hits on You Tube and iTunes.

Like the rappers of the *Y'en A Marre* ('We've Had Enough!') organisation in Senegal, who made such a huge impact during the controversial Presidential elections of 2011 or the

Tunisian MC El General who helped to ignite the so-called Arab Spring, Les Sofas de la République embody a new generation of political thinkers and activists, a youth that has all the communicative power that the internet and digital mobile technology can give but no stake in the official political institutions of their nation, a generation born way after independence and thus immune to the historical justifications used by politicians to stay in power well past their sell-by-date, a peer group who have reached levels of dissatisfaction with the mendacity and corruption of their political leaders that are truly explosive but who retain a passionate faith in African democracy and the need to make it work.

Fifteen to thirty year-olds comprise more than half of the total population of Mali. And yet, thanks to the overriding duty to respect one's elders that is inculcated into all Malian children from birth, fifteen to thirty year olds have had little say in the running of the nation's affairs. The level of education amongst Africa's 'Facebook generation', and their general awareness of what's happening in the world is high. Their frustration with their parents' generation, who won independence, suffered dictatorship, then won back their democracy only to waste it, is extreme. But deep at the heart of this dissatisfaction there lies a realisation that, as the old adage goes, people get the politicians they deserve. It's Les Sofa's ability to criticise themselves and their fellow Malians that makes their discourse so refreshing.

"If we elected an inept government," spokesperson Mohamed 'Ras' Bathily told anthropologist and blogger Bruce Whitehouse, "it is because in the run up to elections we weren't interested in the credibility of the men for whom we were going to vote. Nobody was interested in their social platform, their morality. We just wanted the cash and the t-shirts they were giving away. Even though they took advantage of our ignorance, our poverty and our vulnerability to offer us trifles, we never had this civic reflex to vote for a platform, not for a man."

Music isn't their only weapon. Les Sofas de la République have been organising demonstrations, debates, awareness-raising campaigns and issuing statements about controversial political decisions. Like many rappers in West Africa, most of the group's members are middle class, and some are university educated. Their grasp of political and legal issues is acute, often more so than that of the politicians they criticise. This is reflected in their concerns, the most urgent of which is the need to create a proper civic society in Mali, in which each person is conscious of his or her rights and responsibilities as a citizen in a democracy and the need to fight to defend democratic rights. Les Sofas' latest awareness drive focuses on voter registration, especially amongst the youth.

Ichiaka Bah, aka Amkoullel, is another Malian rapper who believes that music and words should take up arms to defend democracy and promote civic society. "Following the coup d'état, I had some friends, people I've known for years who weren't that militant about what's happening in society," he told me, "but the coup gave them something like an electric shock. We decided to get together and create this collective to take action and express our opposition to the coup. We had this feeling that a real blow had been dealt to democracy and it had been done during a period of popular disillusion. There was a danger that people would accept this coup d'état as something normal, and that's very dangerous, because it was as if, in the collective consciousness, democracy was a failure in Mali. That's not true. It is the representatives and political figures who had been the problem, not the system itself."

Amkoullel formed another rap and direct action collective called 'Plus Jamais Ça' ('Never Again!'). It comprised of rappers, students and friends whose aim was to stimulate the debate around democracy and spread the message that democracy itself had not failed the people, the politicians had failed the people. One of their first events was to create a human chain around the Monument de l'Indépendence in central Bamako, which is situated at the end of one of the city's main thoroughfares, the Boulevard de L'Indépendence. It took place on April 25th 2012, a month after the coup, and attracted over 1,500 people from all kinds of ethnic backgrounds.

"We created the human chain to demonstrate the unity of Mali and say that Mali is indivisible. We organised all this on Facebook and by SMS," Amkoullel explains. "Our phones were bugged at the time. We set up Facebook pages, but ones that other people couldn't use unless they had been invited. We'd organise an action and then everyone went away and told the 20 or 50 or 100 people they know."

Back in the summer of 2011, Amkoullel had written a song called 'SOS' which he recorded with another up and coming Malian rapper called Mylmo, aka Mahamadou Soumbounou. Originally turned onto hip hop by Tatapound, Mylmo won the title of best lyricist at the 2010 Mali Hip Hop Awards. In February 2011 he released an album called '*Vérité*' ('Truth'). *L'Indépendant* newspaper credits him with starting a new trend which they called RAM, or *Le Rap Moraliste* ('Moral Rap').

"'SOS' talks about the disastrous situation in the country," says Amkoullel, "When I wrote it, you could feel this energy, this rage, this frustration in the air. Everyone in Mali, especially in Bamako, felt that something was going to happen. People were unhappy with all the corruption. There was no more trust. It was all going to crack."

Eight months later, in response to the coup and the dire situation in the north, Amkoullel quickly made a video for 'SOS' using news footage of the Islamist takeover supplied by a friend who worked for Reuters. He rush released it on iTunes, Amazon and Soundcloud at the end of May 2012. All proceeds from sales were donated to the Malian Red Cross to relieve the suffering populations in the north. Then came the backlash.

"Once the video was finished, I sent it to the ORTM as usual and they rejected it," he says. "I sent them messages to try and find out why. I mean, in the video, I'm not aggressive against anyone. What's more, the lyrics had been written eight months earlier, so they weren't talking specifically about the situation after the coup, but rather everything that lead up to it. Finally, the ORTM sent me a message saying that it wasn't the right moment to broadcast that kind of video. The junta still controlled ORTM back then. People were frightened to act. When I sent them the video they told me that the Minister of Communications and official government spokesperson had to vet the video first. As if a Malian Minister of State hasn't got anything better to do than look at one of my videos!"

But that wasn't all. Amkoullel began to receive death threats by phone. "Someone phoned and said, 'Yes, we're watching you and we know where to find you, so you'd better calm down or take the consequences.' That was the first message. The second one wasn't from the same person. I get the impression that it was autonomous groups of people who were sending me these messages on their own initiative, rather than following the orders of the junta. This guy said, 'Yeah, you're talking too much. Shut up otherwise you'll disappear and won't even understand a thing." That was a lot clearer! I thought, 'Ok, right, this is really serious!' But then when I got a third message I began to think, "Yeah, yeah, ok, it's the third time now. So are you going to do anything or what??!!'"

If anything, the threats ratcheted up Amkoullel's defiance. "They're nutcases, and you realise that in this country no one is controlling anything. You have to be as mad and as extreme as they are if you're going to stop them. You mustn't just leave them to do what they do. It's out of the question. No one wants to die, but I said to myself that in a way, if they did me over, it might help my struggle even more."

The 'Plus Jamais Ça' association has also met obstacles in the shape of bureaucratic sabotage. The governor of the district where the association was based refused to hand over the authorisations and paperwork that the association needed to become a legal entity. Without them, it can't fundraise or promote events or demonstrate legally. Nonetheless, Amkoullel and his posse carried on regardless, going out into on the poorer neighbourhoods and speaking to the youth about democracy, dictatorship and justice.

"The worse thing in all this is that I came away with the impression that human beings are capable of getting used to anything," he told me in October 2012. "After five or six months we're in danger of accepting the status quo as something normal. Like, as long as they're not shooting or beating people up in the streets, then we're ok, you know? In the north it's different. But we're both imprisoned in our own territory, for different reasons. In the north they've been taken hostage by jihadists, nutters and God freaks. In the south we've been taken hostage by our own army."

With their intellectual power, their courage and their grass roots engagement in the national struggle to keep Mali's diseased democracy alive, Amkoullel, Mylmo, Les Sofas de la République et al represent what might be called the 'conscious' end of the Malian rap scale. Theirs is definitely a *Rap Moraliste* approach. There also exists a younger generation of Malian rap stars, who represent the more mainstream and 'teenie' hip hop end of the spectrum. They also attract a far larger mass-market audience than the Rap Moraliste activists. Amongst these younger MCs, two names stand out; Iba One and Sidiki Diabaté, the eldest son of no lesser person than kora virtuoso Toumani Diabaté, one of the most famous Malian musicians in the world.

"Today Malian rappers, including my son Sidiki Diabaté, can fill stadiums," Toumani told me with obvious pride. "His rap group were nominated the best beat makers in Malian hip hop. He himself plays the kora and so he makes traditional music mixed with hip hop. He's a pupil at the Malian music conservatory. For the feast of Tabeski they did a gig in the biggest stadium in Mali, the *26 Mars*. Thank God there are still musicians who can fill stadiums."

"You can't imagine a rap movement that has the power and the force of the rap movement in Mali today," Toumani continues. "Iba One and Sidiki Diabaté, they're the number one rappers in Mali. Amkoullel and Tatapound are guys that I know and respect. They're intellectuals. But the messages of Iba One and Sidiki are even clearer and sharper than theirs, more direct. Their lyrics talk about the ills of our society, the problems but at the same time their music is very rhythmic, in the true spirit of Malian music."

Sidiki and Iba One did a track with Gaspi and Memo All Star called 'On Veut La Paix' ('We Want Peace') with a swinging ragga feel, honeyed R&B vocals and a delivery that is noticeably mellower than either Amkoullel or Les Sofas. This is perhaps the reason why the posse were invited to perform the song live over playback on ORTM, prime time. On footage of the performance, Sidiki's kora tinkles like a soothing fountain in the background. The gestures are as globalised as a Big Mac. Nonetheless the messages hit home; *'Mali is one and indivisible!', 'We make peace not war or hate!', 'We want peace!'*

Conscious rap, teenie rap, Bambara rap, Tamashek rap, Songhoi rap, Manding rap; rap in Mali is huge and varied. The simple beat and flow, the very simplicity that scares the musical old guard, is rap's strength, allowing the genre to propagate in places where money to buy instruments or the opportunity to learn millennial musical techniques and oral poetry don't exist. All you need is a mic and a beat box and you're in business. A sharp flow of words captured on a mobile phone and uploaded to the net and you're on your way.

Africa has embraced the immediacy and simplicity of rap and is turning it into a weapon of social consciousness and awareness-raising. And if the role models are Jay-Z, Tupac Shakur, Eminem, Notorious B.I.G and Beyoncé, with all their ghetto fab conceits, Africa has taken their rap and made it its own; a raw and youthful voice that can travel far and wide using the Internet and the mobile phone, tools that the elders have barely begun to understand.

The rage and sincerity in the delivery of Ramses or Master Soumy from Les Sofas de la République, of Amkoullel or El General and the MCs of Y'en A Marre, is the only stamp of authenticity that their young listeners really need, an authenticity that they so rarely feel in the speeches of their political leaders. The new manifestoes of Africa's emerging generations are rapped in rhyme and as such reach so much further than cold words on a page.

That's what the Islamists don't understand. Without music, how can you rally people, communicate with them, send out messages, nurture social consciences or raise awareness in Africa. "Iyad Ag Ghali has gone too far," said Ahmed Ag Kaedi, the guitarist from Amanar, whose equipment was burned in Kidal by Ansar ud-Dine. "And if he really wants to impose his Shari'a, I think he would be better off using artists and musicians to get his message across… ha ha ha. It's hard to get a message heard in Mali without music."

11. Without music, Mali will die

The musicians and cultural activists of Mali speak

During almost every one of the 24 interviews I conducted whilst researching this book, the passage in which every interviewee excelled in terms of passion and eloquence occurred when I asked them to respond to the MUJAO ban on music in the north, issued by decree on August 23rd 2012. So, by way of concluding this examination of music in Mali under fire, here are those responses, given to me in October 2012, in the darkest days of the jihadi takeover of northern Mali. I hope you'll agree, they say it all:

Cheikh Tidiane Seck:
"Music guides the whole of our society. The proof is that the griot became so institutional. He was like a judge, a lawyer, a federator, who calmed quarrels in the old days. Everything in Mali involves music, even funerals. Music regulates the life of a Malian, from ancient days until today. When I heard that the MUJAO had declared all music forbidden except Quranic chanting in the name of Islam, I wanted to go up there myself. We musicians… go up there, and sacrifice our lives. They can't take that away from us."

Rokia Traore:
"I try not to think about it too much. It just would get me nowhere. Right now, I have to work and do as much as I can, because I reckon that the mere fact I can still work is a great fortune. Under shari'a, it would mean that people like me could no longer live in Mali. Obviously, I'm a Muslim. I've always been a believer, but shari'a law is not my thing. I don't believe in it and if it has to exist in my country, I could no longer work in Mali. I would cease to exist in one way or another. And at the same, Malian culture would cease to

exist. I hope that Mali won't be another global catastrophe in cultural terms."

Manny Ansar, director of the Festival in the Desert:
"Everything is transmitted in Mali through music, through poetry. We enjoy life through music. The MUJAO can exist but not among this people. And I don't see how, in the 21st century, they'll manage to occupy this entire territory without the support of the people who live there. So, that declaration of theirs, instead of making me panic, at least it tells me that we're dealing with people who don't know what they're doing, who aren't serious and who won't win. Because they're aiming for Utopia. They don't understand the culture that they're operating in and they don't try and understand it either. And most importantly, they're not in harmony with the population."

Ahmed Ag Kaedi from the group Amanar:
"When I heard about the MUJAO ban, I was scared for music. Because modern Touareg music wasn't born that long ago, and I was scared it was going to die. If it dies, I'll die with it, because playing music is the only thing I can do."

Amadou Bagayoko:
"It is as if they were trying to annihilate Malian culture generally. Already, when a child is born, on the seventh day there's the baptism and the griots come to sing praises. That's happened since time immemorial. And at weddings there was always dance music. And when people went into the fields, there were also musicians who accompanied the farmers. There's also music for the hunters. So that's why I say that banning music… it isn't a possibility. Because if one forbade music, it would be like eradicating Malian culture itself.

In the life of nations, there are always moments of hardship and catastrophe. I consider this to be one of those moments, something that has happened, spontaneously, to come and stop the onward march of life. But I don't think it is a situation that will endure, because the country has been secular for a long time. Mali isn't just a country of Muslims, there are also Christians and Animists. So it's not by strong-arming that one can stop all of that. I don't think so. As for the idea of stopping music… well, ha ha, that would be very complicated! There would be no weddings, no baptisms. We don't speak Arabic. What would we do? What would we say? We can't only listen to what is said in Arabic, we must listen to things to that are said in our own language, in our own tradition. That's very important."

Adam Thiam, journalist:
"As a Malian who believes in freedom, I was shocked by the declaration of the MUJAO. It was even hard to believe. But I grew up in a very Islamicised family. My father was a marabout, devoted to the Quran. So I'm rather familiar with that kind of restriction. But as a modern Malian, I was shocked. Up in the north, music is one of the rare pleasures in a very hard environment, with a very poor economy. For example, in Gao, the takamba is like the blues was for the blacks on the plantations of the American south.

If we lose the musical productivity that we have now, we will have lost Mali's biggest ambassador outside the country. Malian music has driven the marketing of the country, its image, these past twenty years. So any law that represses musical creativity in Mali today deprives it of its biggest weapon for marketing and promotion in the world at large.

I also think that music is the first ingredient of our social capital. In Rwanda, for example, I noticed that apart from a few bands that were more or less set up by humanitarian organisations, people don't sing. It is different in Mali. If MUJAO came to Bamako and deprived the people of their sounou or whatever else, they would really be depriving them of the most effective tool of socialisation."

Bassekou Kouyaté:
"If there is no music, there will be no Mali. Mali is known through its music. It is a cradle for music. What are we going to do if there's no music? Just sit here all day looking at people go by? In my opinion, those people want to destroy this country and all that we have achieved since ages. They're bandits. Honestly, we can't go on like that. We have to find a solution. We need the Western countries to come and rescue us and get rid of those people. They aren't even Malians. They can't come and colonise us all over again. We want our democracy. We really want it back."

Toumani Diabaté:
"It is sad what is happening, it is sad and unacceptable and unimaginable too. One trusts in God and prays for this problem to go away. Mali has never known this before. I ask the whole world to become ambassadors of Mali and to help bring peace back, because it is not just a problem that concerns only Mali. It's also a problem for the rest of the world. So we must never give a possibility to people who call themselves the emissaries of God or whatever. We are all religious and it is not for anybody else to give us lessons about religion. Religion is faith. We were born into it, with parents who were Muslims. So we don't need to be told what to do by anybody coming from the outside. We're a peaceful people with a cultural tradition that is very big and very powerful. That culture is our petrol. That culture is our diamonds, our mineral wealth. So we'll never accept that people come and try to destroy history, try to hide and destroy the heritage of your country. We'll never accept that.

I'm taking this opportunity to thank the entire European, American, Asian music business for its support for the cause of Malian music. And the people who come and learn music here, or even people who buy tickets to go and see the different Malian musicians in concert, I take this opportunity say thanks and bravo to you all, and may the struggle continue.

I'm not stopping. I'm rehearsing with my band right now and I'm making use of this fallow time to prepare a new record, which I'll begin to record very soon. I'm a musician in a line of 71 generations of musicians, kora players, from father to son, so the only thing I can do in life is that. It is my breadwinner. I'm not a footballer. I know that I'll never play in the Stade de France or at Wembley. The only thing I do, which is my destiny, is to play music. And I'm an ambassador of my culture, of the culture of my country. I represent a culture and a tradition that is very old, over seven centuries old. So it's out of the question that I abandon all that to do something else. I can only do that and I will continue doing that work, as will my children and my family. I sincerely hope that we'll continue doing the work of music, by the grace of God."

Rhissa (not his real name) – musician from Kidal:
"What Iyad, MUJAO and the others who are in Timbuktu are imposing hasn't pleased anyone, to tell you the truth. There are those who go along with it because they have to, or because they haven't understood it. That's what is happening. Many people have gone away so they can do what they want. You have to study religion to know it well. It is not something you can use for your own ends. And if you want to impose it on people, you have to do it with them, you have to be kind to them. But in their case, they just arrived and then boom! There's nothing left to discuss. They've consulted no one and sought the opinion of no one. It was forced on people. Tamashek culture without music isn't possible. I can tell that today, it is just a form of chaos that has arrived. And I don't think it'll last long."

Amkoullel:

"I don't give a f**k what they say. Unfortunately they're in a position of force to impose what they've declared on part of the country, but that, I hope, will only be temporary. We won't let them get away with it. What they think is their own business. And we never waited for them in order to be Muslims. Mali is a secular country, tolerant, where everyone declares their religion according to their feeling, and in any case, they know that a Mali without music is an impossibility.

Even before the Almoravid invasions, with the penetration of the Muslim religion here in Mali, the culture of tolerance already existed in the old rituals, what we call the Animist religions, even if I don't like that term very much. But in the old religions there was respect for the other. Because, in Mali, when you're little you're told that if a stranger comes to your house, they're worth more than you. If you only have one bed in which to sleep, you must sleep on the floor and give your only bed to the stranger. So there's nothing more tolerant and open and respectful of others than Malian culture. And it isn't religion that brought all of that. It was there before. It mixed with Islam when religion arrived. And basically religion is tolerant.

The problem is that those Islamists who come, their aim is to destroy all reference, all memory and history. That's why they attack the mausoleums. That's why they have to destroy culture and music. Because when you destroy all the references of a people, its memory which is preserved in its museums, its monuments, its music and culture, well then, it's like they don't have a past any more, and then you can replace what it had with what you're proposing. That's the first stage of alienation, but the problem for them is that it is going to be very difficult because we live in a world in which new technologies have developed. They're in a country in which there are artists who are committed to protest, who speak up. There are rappers and also others, so there are many ways in which to fight against those people."

Yehia from the group Takambo Super 11:
"Music is so important in Gao. The people of Gao love their takamba. They don't have another style that they love so much. So if they're forbidden to play and listen to takamba in Gao, really, they have nothing left. And many of us live only from playing music. Imagine, you live from your guitar but if you bring it with you eastwards past Mopti, they'll take it and destroy it."

Vieux Farka Touré:
"Really and truly, I don't think those guys have anything to do with Islam. You can't even call them Islamists. They're jokers, you know. For them it is all about weapons and drugs. They're just opportunists, not Islamists. By trying to destroy music they want to break people's spirits, so that they can control them better. But I don't think it is possible. Music is something very powerful in the human spirit, so it is not just by shaking your finger than you can destroy it. Music has a big impact on all of us because it provides a place for us to come together. It is our meeting place, where we're happy, where there's friendship and companionship. Everything happens around music. It is life. It is as if they're attacking part of our life."

Nina Walet Intallou, female member of the Transitional Council for the State of Azawad:
"An attack on music is an attack on women in our society. Because music is so often a women's affair. For Tamashek women, everything happens around music, the tindé, the violin, *iswat* at night. [Iswat is a form of poetry sung by both women and men in Touareg culture.] The young girls, when they perform iswat, that's when the youth come and find their partners or their future fiancées.

It is an attack on the soul of our society. When the MUJAO declare that all music is forbidden except praise singing, it is a way to kill our culture. No one agrees with that. They're killing our culture and abusing us. The Arabs don't want us to talk about that, saying that we're racists, but we'll do everything to keep the only real wealth that we possess, which is our culture. It is an attempt to oppress Amazigh culture. And all those Islamists, as they couldn't do it by inter-marrying etc., they're trying to do it with Islam. To kill our culture."

Cheick Ag Tilia from the group Tamikrest:
"Unless I'm much mistaken, music is not forbidden in Islam. It isn't a sin for you to play music, or sing to express your truth. The Touareg people without music would be like, to give you an example, someone whose face has been completely burnt, or someone who doesn't have a face at all. He doesn't have a personality. It is like a people without any personality or soul. But we're still playing music. We're going to rehearse at Tinzawaten, at the frontier between Algeria and Mali. We'll carry on. At all the gigs we've done in Tinzawaten, people have come from everywhere, crossing the border from Mali to see us. But I also know young people who are supposedly in Ansar ud-dine who still listen to their music when they're alone, no problem. They smoke their cigarettes as they've always done… but only amongst themselves."

Fadimata Walet Oumar also known as **Disco** from the Tartit Ensemble:
"I felt that this is the end. The game's up. Because for us, the Touareg, music is an essential element in our lives. And if we're told that we cannot make music it means that a part of ourselves has been cut out. For us, that's an impossibility. Music is something that touches the deepest part of us, and it would be as if they've cut off our capacity to breathe. Because traditionally, every evening we play tindé, we play

the imzad, we play the teherdent. We live like that. It is our life. It is our roots. So if they cut that off from us, it is as if they've cut away everything. There'd be no point in carrying on living any more. And if I shout out about it the MUJAO will cut my tongue out… ha ha ha!!!

In reality, it's not just music, it is the freedom of women that they want to destroy. Because as you well know, in our culture, women are almost freer than anywhere else on earth. So that's why they want to forbid music, dancing and all that. We'll never agree to it. They'll have to kill us first. When they arrived in the desert, they saw how we lived. In fact, they already knew how we lived. We're Muslims. We pray, we believe in God but that doesn't stop us partying. That doesn't stop us dancing or singing. But then we'll say our prayers. And we will wear a veil, but not in the way they want us to. They're trying to impose laws from the 18th century on us. Maybe they're acceptable in Saudi Arabia or someplace else but we've never accepted those laws. And we never will accept them. I think they want to rob us of the ability to be free women, to be women that can speak and be heard, to keep us like they keep their own women; locked up without any rights.

Without free women, without strong women, there'll be no Touareg and there'll be no Tamashek culture. It would mean that our culture ends right there. And our life as Touareg would end too. Because it would be another life for us, a completely different one to the life we've known. For millennia we've lived like that. Millennia! Since beginning of time we've always lived like that. And it is not a little group of MUJAO who'll change that life we've lived. We'll never return to the country if it stays like that. We'll remain in exile for the rest of our lives."

Ismaiel Ag Mohammed also known as **Massiwa**, organiser of the Camel Fair in Tessalit:
"Tamashek culture without music isn't possible. But I hope that it is all a nightmare that will go away. People hope that it'll pass. Because it's very difficult for a people to live like that. Music plays a very important role in Tamashek culture, and in daily life. Music is a large component of society. It is true that they've said that all music is forbidden. And people are obliged to follow what they're ordered to do, because they have no choice. But the people aren't happy at all. They don't want that. It is very difficult, very difficult for the people.

Ibrahim Ag Ahmed also known as **Pino**, bassist with the group Terakaft:
"Music cannot be disassociated from the image of the Tamashek people. Why? Because in this huge expanse of desert, man is nostalgic. He's homesick. He has the sky and the stars for a roof, and he has the whole desert for his house. So, on his dromedary, he covers hundreds of kilometres looking for water and all that. Music has to be part of his daily life. So he makes a traditional flute out of wood. He helps to create the tindé. The Touareg guitar comes from the tindé. So that's it. He can't live without that. It's not possible. You feel that everywhere. You hear it even. When you stop in the desert, what you'll miss is music, of course. In a moment of nostalgia, women poets can't help themselves from singing about that sadness, that arid bitter desert. It gives them the best of themselves. They're at peace in that. They see nature. It is their circle of life. You can't take it from the Touareg, it is not possible."

Jamal (not his real name) – musician from Kidal:
"Well, that's what I'm telling you, music is banned everywhere. In any case, we're in the shit. No one wants it, but that's how it is. We have no choice because we're dealing with people who are armed, who are deep into the system.

You don't know what to do any more. All you can do is observe."

Cheick Oumar Sissoko, film director and former Malian Minister of Culture:
"Music is the most important part of our heritage. Because music is memory. Music is tradition. There isn't a single tradition in our country that isn't magnified by music. That music is represented at weddings, baptisms, circumcision ceremonies, funerals, harvest ceremonies… and social cohesion, national cohesion. Music provides the rhythm of our lives so if there isn't any music, it means death.

But there is resistance to all they're trying to do today, even in Gao, Timbuktu and Kidal. Like yesterday in Douentza, people went into a bar to drink, perhaps even alcohol. In the end, they were arrested and whipped. The owner of the bar fled. But if there was no resistance, that wouldn't be possible. And people continue to claim their right to watch TV, to smoke cigarettes, to listen to the music of their choice. It is that spirit that will lead to a mobilisation in the towns when there is an attack from the outside. Because the youth up there are organising themselves, you know? The youth have even confronted them, even if just with their hands and sticks, to say it is too much. And often we received messages that we broadcast through our Free Radios that we're sick of what's happening. And that's risky because we know that the Islamists have their representatives here in Bamako and they could send back the names of the people concerned."

Afel Bocoum:
"Yes, but isn't Quranic singing also music? Malian musicians also sing for the Prophet Mohammed. We sing about religion. We sing about men. We sing about the animals. We sing about the earth. But isn't singing for a religion also making music? What about singing for the animals. Because

the Muslims up there in the north cannot live without nature. They can't live without their animals.

Their ambition isn't Islam. It is something else. My view of it is that it's a chaos that has been born. I don't see it as a religious movement, in the name of God, or in the name of one or another religion. We're not a religious country, we're a secular country. Why start telling us about religion now, today. The old people of Timbuktu have no need to go to school now to learn about Islam. It's just a chaos, an uncontrollable chaos. It is an occupation that has nothing to do with the Muslim religion."

12. In the name of Mali

The intellectuals and writers of Mali appeal to the armed groups in the north

On Friday May 4th 2012, militiamen from Ansar ud-Dine and Al Qaida in the Islamic Maghreb desecrated the tomb of Sidi Mahmoud Ben Omar Mohamed Aqit, a 15th century jurist and one of the most revered of Timbuktu's 333 saints. A few days later, a movement of Malian writers and cultural activists called *Malivaleurs* issued the following statement:

"In the name of the cultural heritage of Mali, patiently and gradually built over centuries and millennia. In the name of the Touareg scholars, inheritors of the city of es-Souk. In the name of empire builders, of wise men, writers and Manding explorers. In the name of those who performed rites, rituals and customs.

In the name of the merchants of the savannah who built up the great trading cities and the economies of pre-colonial times. In the name of those who produced the goods that were traded. In the name of the Donso hunters who founded villages and traditions of self-defence. In the name of the artists and craftsmen of bygone times, of the men of memory who created our historical chronicles and literary heritage.

In the name of the traditions of intellectual and military resistance that we developed over the centuries, every time our land found itself under threat. In the name of the social fabric, seemingly so well woven together, of the family and community relations built by 52 years of interaction within this Republic. In the name of our contemporaries, all you who have made a contribution to this material and spiritual heritage.

We say to the forces of occupation that Mali's heart beats in every one of its children! Mali's heart beats in every one of us! We are telling those armed groups to take care! We are telling them that they should fear the combined riposte of the armed forces and internal resistance.

We say to the forces of occupation that they should treat our heritage with care. That heritage is made up of goods held in common, both material and spiritual, which belong to all and which have been inherited by the entire community. That heritage comprises the manuscripts which are the pride and singularity of Timbuktu, Mali and Africa. It comprises the shrines and mausoleums, the old habitations and streets, all the built infrastructure of our ancient cities, the historic and cultural sites and all the knowledge that lies within them. That heritage is also everything being built at the present moment, for future generations, that bears the mark of our culture. That heritage comprises all cultural goods and products, either finished or still in the process of being created by the writers, creative people and visionaries of today.

That heritage comprises the social and political charters, modelled on the Kurukan Fuga, which bind our communities together. Those charters lay down the foundations of social and inter-community relations. Non-material, quintessential, those links are the basis of civil behaviour, of peace and understanding between individuals, groups, neighbours and people from different backgrounds.

This heritage consists of all the marks of identity, whether they're monuments, cultural sites or places of human interest. In this regard, we protest vigorously against the degradation suffered by the Gina Dogon monument in Douentza and by the Alfarouk monument and the mausoleums of the saints in Timbuktu. The Republic of Mali is secular. We categorically condemn any attack against cultural diversity and ask all heritages and cultures to be respected without exception.

The Malivaleurs Movement, the Malian Coalition for Cultural Diversity, the Collective of Malian Writers and PEN-Mali, la Medina, Balanise and all cultural activists send out this appeal to the MNLA, Ansar ud-Dine, AQMI and the other armed movements to respect all these heritages, which belong to all humanity.

The nation must draw on these heritages in its efforts to promote dialogue. First, and above all, dialogue! In the name of reason, wisdom and intelligence!"

13. "Only God can protect you"

Why do some Muslims want to destroy shrines and mausoleums?

Practising Muslims begin their prayers with the *shahada*; the simplest possible declaration of their faith. In Arabic it goes *"la 'ilaha 'illà I-Lah, Muhammadur rasulu I'Lah."* In English: "There is no god but God, Muhammad is the messenger of God."

This declaration expresses the essence of what Muslims call the 'Oneness' or, more clumsily, the 'Unicity' of God. In Arabic the word is *'Tawhid'*. What it means is that God is one, indivisible, unique, above and beyond all that is created. No person or thing can share in the godliness of God. No person or thing can be His partner on earth. No person or thing can be worshipped in the place of God, or as a symbol of God. No person or thing can be like God, of God, part of God, or be said to possess any of His characteristics. Ardent belief in God's Oneness denies divinity or sanctity to saints, tombs, relics, charms and amulets or 'holy' works of art. To worship or invoke any of these as a conduit to God would be idolatry, and idolatry is the only unpardonable sin in the Quran:

(Quran 4:48) *"Allah forgiveth not that partners should be set up with Him; but he forgiveth everything else, to whom He pleaseth; to set up partners with Allah is to devise a sin most heinous indeed."*

All practicing Muslims are on a path leading to God and Oneness, but a Muslim who has chosen the Sufi way will use various methods to navigate that path that are not necessarily found in the Quran or the sayings and actions of the Prophet Mohammed, collectively known as the *hadith*. Those Sufi methods might involve *zikr*, or the musical repetition of God's name. They might involve dance or movement or other means of bodily and mental purification such as trance, ecstasy, abnegation or incense. The Sufi might also claim that God can be felt or even reached through the veneration of shrines or the tombs of saints. God is deemed to be present in a *zaouia*, the place where the members of a brotherhood or *tariqa* gather together to teach and carry out their observances. A Sufi learns from a teacher or master, who imparts knowledge not only by transmitting the word of God as written down in the Quran but also by leading an exemplary life and giving off a divine aura which infuses his pupil with God's light. The master can thus become an object of veneration in himself.

A Sufi believes that through prayer, fasting, purification, zikr, trance, ecstasy, learning and spiritual 'intoxication', it is possible to go beyond the divisions of earthly existence and become suffused with the Oneness of God *in this life*. In other words, Sufism is more of a mystical journey towards selflessness, Oneness and Godliness than a rational prescribed system of belief and behaviour. It is guided more by intuition and emotional connection than by reason. That intuitive emotional approach gives the Sufi some latitude to integrate local customs into his religious practice and colour his devotion to Allah with the tint of local cultures. Some even argue that without the 'flexibility' of Sufism and its ability to integrate with varied cultures, Islam would not have taken hold over so vast a territory stretching from Morocco in the west to Malaysia in the east.

Faith colours culture and vice versa. In parts of West Africa and the Maghreb, Islam's interaction with local beliefs, customs and rhythms has nurtured culturally unique devotional phenomena like the Gnawa or Aissawa brotherhoods in Morocco or the Baye Fall in Senegal. Although constantly nurtured by contact with the Middle East, the colours of West African Islam are essentially home grown.

On the other hand, a Muslim who has espoused the Salafi way abhors all the esoteric innovations or *bid'ah* of the Sufis. For him, the Quran, the hadīth and the example of the Prophet Mohammed are all that any true Muslim needs to study in order to live a righteous life. The Salafi's models are the *as-Salaf as-Saaleh*, the 'righteous predecessors' or forefathers of the Muslim faith. For him, any rituals, laws or habits that have been 'invented' and added to the beliefs and practice of the righteous models in the twelve centuries since the time of the Prophet are mostly unnecessary, often unlawful and very possibly sinful.

Although the words 'Salafist' or 'Salafiya' have become loaded in recent years and used to denote groups or sects with a particularly hard line, rigorous or even violent world view, many Sunni Muslim scholars will tell you that a true Salafi is not a member of a sect. Neither is he someone who necessarily judges the world or his fellow Muslims harshly. He's simply a devotee who follows the original path of Allah, as set down by his Prophet Mohammed and the small group who rallied around him at the dawn of Islam. In other words, for many, a Salafi is nothing other than a true Muslim. Some Salafiya however believe that righteous and possibly violent jihad is necessary, not only against *kuffar* or 'unbelievers', in other words Christians, Jews, Buddhists, Zoroastrians, animists and any other non-Muslim, but also against Muslims who have strayed from the true path and have introduced blasphemous 'innovations' into Islam. Sufis, with their esoteric practices, are often held up as the guiltiest in this regard.

In West and North Africa, where Sufi brotherhoods like the Tijaniya, the Qadiriya and the Mourides have been overlaying their own locally grown rites and practices on top of the basic tenets of Sunni Islam for centuries, many Salafis see a vast sea of blasphemous innovation and esoteric perversion of Islam. The relative freedom of women in comparison to their counterparts in the Middle East, the vestiges of pre-Islamic beliefs in local spiritual life, the use of music and dance in devotional practice, the adherence to the Maliki school of Islamic law, rather than the stricter and more rigorous Hanbali school that prevails in Saudi Arabia, the veneration of saints, shrines and holy relics, the lax application of Islamic law and the secular legal and political constitutions of modern West African states, all of these are anathema to the Salafi.

The spread of Islam into West Africa was always a slow and haphazard affair. It started with an influx of Muslim traders from the north in the 8th century. At first these traders were barely tolerated by local rulers and often kept apart from local populations. With time however, their literacy, their numeracy, their scientific knowledge and trading skills became prized. Small isolated Muslim communities grew into entire neighbourhoods, villages and towns. Islam was often an urban phenomenon, promoted by a wealthy merchant class who considered their faith to be rational, modern, progressive and sophisticated in comparison to what they saw as the crude, primitive, even savage nature of indigenous spiritual beliefs.

Nonetheless the spread of the faith was slow. When he visited the Niger bend in 1352, the great geographer and traveller Ibn Battuta was gratified to find that the inhabitants of the Malian empire had “a zeal for learning the Quran by heart.” But despite the generally faithful observance of Islam, he was shocked to see that men and women mixed freely and that “their women show no bashfulness before men, and do no veil themselves.” Ibn Battuta attended a ceremony led by King Mansa Souleyman, the great Mansa Musa’s successor, which started with Muslim prayers but then “degenerated” with the arrival of dancers dressed as birds. This, the eminent geographer believed, was insulting to his faith. He did not appreciate the fact that the King had to engage his commoners, many of whom still held on to old Animist beliefs.

By the late 18th century, when the Scotsman Mungo Park made the first of his famous journeys from the Atlantic coast of West Africa into the heart of what is now modern day Mali, the lands he passed through featured a patchwork of Islamic and Animist mini-states, living side by side, often fighting with each other. The Bambara people, for example, who now dominate Malian society and politics, were generally non-Muslims in Park's time, whereas the then more powerful neighbouring kingdom of Massina had embraced Islam.

At various times in history great waves of Islamic reformation have risen up and descended on the Sahel to reassert 'true' Islam, starting with the *al-Murabitun* or Almoravids, an 11th century Berber reform movement that began in what is now the Western Sahara and spread its vigorous Islamic orthodoxy throughout North Africa, southern Spain and the Ghana empire. Along the way the al-Murabitun jihadis founded the city of Marrakech and bequeathed the word 'marabout' to posterity.

In the early 19th century, the Fulani kingdom of Hamdallahi, which means "Praise God", took control of a large territory adjoining the Niger, including the town of Timbuktu. There they imposed a very strict form of shari'a law, which forbade men and women to mix, banned tobacco and music and forced the local population to attend prayers at the mosque.

More recently, at dawn of the colonial era, the great scholar, fighter and religious reformer Cheikh Al Hadj Oumar Tall spread jihad throughout West Africa under the banner of the Sufi Tijanniya order. Whilst studying in Mecca in the 1820s, Hadj Oumar Tall's genius as a scholar and devotee had impressed the founder of the Tijani order Cheikh Ahmed Tijani and he invested Tall with the position of *khalifa* or representative in West Africa. Cheikh Tijani's chief pupil Sidi Al-Ghali ordered Hadj Oumar Tall to "cleanse the lands of the stench of paganism." In 1852, after receiving a blessing for his mission in a dream from both Cheikh Tijani and the Prophet Mohammed himself, Hadj Oumar Tall launched jihad against the Bambara and Massina kingdoms, founding the Toucouleur Empire in the process. He died in 1864.

So the imposition or re-imposition of the 'true' Islamic faith by force of arms in West Africa and the Sahel is nothing new. Religion in that part of the world has long been synonymous with conquest, power and politics, just as it has in Europe and elsewhere.

What is new about groups like AQIM, MUJAO and Ansar ud-Dine is the Salafi rigor of its leaders, a rigor that is alien to the mainstream Sufism of West African Islam. Unlike the Qadiri Sufism of the Hamdallahi kingdom or the Tijani Sufism of Hadj Oumar Tall, both of which could be stern and puritanical in their own way, this Salafi orthodoxy is entirely foreign. It has no affinity with the Sufi saints of West Africa and the traditions that they helped to build. It is the 21st century manifestation of an archconservative approach to Islam that was born in Saudi Arabia over two centuries ago, and has roots that go even further back in time.

It would be foolish to deny that a philosophical foundation of sorts underpins the more extreme activities of the Salafiyya in northern Mali. The pick-wielding militiamen who destroyed the shrine of Sidi Mahmoud in Timbuktu and so many other venerable buildings and structures since had no doubt that they were doing right by God and man. Their destruction was not blind in their own eyes. The very existence of Sidi Mahmoud's shrine and the popular belief that its sanctity could protect the people of Timbuktu was a perfect example to their minds of the very lie that binds the people of northern Mali to their ignorance, their subservience and their poverty.

For a succinct, chatty and easily understandable explanation of the Salafi aversion to shrines and 'idols', you could do worse than listen to the talk by the American Muslim teacher Yusuf Estes on YouTube. His subject is the *Wahabiya*, the followers of Muhammad ibn Abd-al Wahhab, an 18th century preacher from the Najd or desert interior of the Arabian Peninsula. Abd al-Wahab was a brilliant scholar who had memorised the Quran before he was a teenager and who insisted that a Muslim had the right to learn and draw wisdom from all the different schools of Islamic jurisprudence – Maliki, Hanbali, Shafi'i and Hanafi. This was dangerous talk at the time and Abd al-Wahab was deemed to be a troublesome radical by many of the more traditional religious leaders of his day.

Abd al-Wahab's basic claim was that Muslim scholars should have greater intellectual freedom to study the religious texts and sources rather than blindly accepting the precepts of one school of thought or another. He also felt that many of the rules and codes of the Quran and the Hadith had become rusty and distorted through misuse over the centuries. He urged his people to go back to basics and adopt a strict and unyielding application of Islam's founding precepts. This rigorous approach found favour with Muhammad ibn Saud, Abd al-Wahab's brother in law and ruler of the Saudi dynasty, who was busy conquering neighbouring kingdoms in the second half of the 18th century. Conquest helped Abd al-Wahab's ideas to spread and become orthodoxy throughout the Najd and beyond. Two centuries later, those same teachings have become the spiritual and religious foundation of the kingdom of Saudi Arabia.

In Yusuf Estes' talk on the Wahabiya, he begins by explaining that *wahab* is an Arabic word meaning to 'bestow' or 'give'. "If you say *al wahab*, you must be very careful," he warns. "You just said Allah's name. Allah is *al Wahab*, he is the The Bestower." He goes on to say that Muhammad ibn

Abd al-Wahab came to the conclusion that "the people of his time were making a grave mistake. I use the right word too 'cause they were worshipping graves. They were literally going to graves and calling on dead people to help them. Righteous people, good people… but they're dead! And even if they were alive what could they do? They could only make law for you. Nobody's got any magic. You ask Allah to solve these impossible situations and he can do it. And that's what he was telling the people."

The destruction of the holy sites of Islam by the followers of Abd al-Wahab began in 1806 when the army of the House of Saud captured the city of Mecca and destroyed shrines and mausoleums in the Jannat al-Baqi cemetery, where many of the Prophet Mohammed's family members and early devotees were buried. As-Saud and his soldiers even tried to destroy the Prophet's tomb. Several years later the Ottomans regained control of the holy cities of Mecca, Medina and Ta'if, and the Saudi army was pushed back into the desert interior. The Turks rebuilt many of the shrines, lavishly and beautifully. A century later, in 1925, Abdel Aziz Ibn Saud, the new ruler of the House of Saud, rose up with his army of desert-hardened Bedouin soldiers and recaptured the holy cities. They called these warriors of God *Ikhwan* or 'the Brothers' and their declared goal was to restore the one and only pure faith in the lands of the Prophet. When they entered Medina they destroyed the structures in the al-Baqi cemetery once again. In Mecca they reduced the tomb of the Prophet's first wife Khadijah as well as those of his mother and grandfather to rubble. Many other sites of historical importance also bit the dust.

This annihilation of Arabia's built heritage has continued ever since, spurred by the need to create space in the old centres of the holy cities for the ever growing numbers of pilgrims who visit every year. Over 300 buildings and structures relating directly to the Prophet and his companions, including Mohammed's house in Medina, have been razed to the ground and car parks, shopping malls, glitzy marble esplanades and in one case, a public toilet, have taken their place.

At the heart of this destruction lies an adherence to Oneness and Tawhid taken to literalist extremes. It is based on the firm belief that God is One and that all men are equal under him. Men should not be venerated in lieu of Allah or as a conduit to Allah, not during their lives and especially not after they have died. Tombs should be modest affairs, barely visible above the ground.

A passage in the Sahih Al Bukhari, one of the six major hadith of Sunni Islam, often quoted by the Salafiya, recounts that the Prophet once said that Allah had damned Jews and Christians because they had treated the tombs of their prophets as places of worship. "Certainly, those who came before you considered the tombs of their prophets and pious men amongst them as places of prayer. Therefore do not treat tombs as if they were mosques, for I forbid it," the Prophet Mohammed was reported to have said in another hadith. He also commanded Ali, his cousin and companion, to reduce any tomb he saw that had been surmounted by a statue or edifice, back down to ground level.

Legal authority for the destruction of mausoleums also rests on the judgements or *fatwas* of the 13th century Kurdish jurist Ibn Taymiyah, who Salafis and Wahabis often hold up as *Cheikh al-Islam*; the greatest scholar Islam has ever known. Ibn Taymiyah issued several fatwas condemning the worship of graves and shrines that were refuted by other scholars almost as soon as they were issued. Abd al-Wahab later explained that Ibn Taymiyah had condemned unbelievers, rather than tomb worshippers as such. "It is *halal* [permissible] to kill and confiscate those who make mediators of prophets or masters," al-Wahab wrote. In the mind of the unyielding Wahabi, these words condemn most Sufis to death.

Interestingly, Ibn Taymiyah himself was buried in a Sufi cemetery in Damascus in 1328 AD, although he often made judgements against Sufism and condemned it for straying from the straight path. The whole cemetery was destroyed during the French protectorate in the 1920s and the land cleared to make way for the expanded campus of Damascus University and a maternity hospital. However, King Abdel Aziz as-Saud of Saudi Arabia personally intervened to save Ibn Taymiyah's grave from destruction. It still exists, hidden away behind the hospital buildings, neglected, surrounded by weeds, but intact.

For the Ikhwan soldiers of Ibn Saud, theological motivations were intensified by a species of cultural war; a struggle between the stark and stripped desert mentality of the Najd, or harsh arid interior, and the more sensuous and indulgent culture of the Hijaz, the populated coastal regions of Saudi Arabia where the tombs and shrines of the revered dead had long been worshipped before the Saudi takeover of the 1920s and 1930s. Wahabism is Islam without artistry or adornment, as stark and severe as the barebacked hills and geometric horizons of the inner Arabian Desert. It suits a certain isolated desert mentality, one that is naturally suspicious of, even averse to the gentler sensuality of more fertile regions or the open-minded cosmopolitanism of coasts and ports with old connections to the wider world. Its appeal to a cosmopolitan and relatively well-to-do merchant class in Mali and West Africa is therefore contradictory in many ways. For them, Wahabism is progressive and has the added advantage of being a foreign novelty, untainted by the faithful but 'backward' hearts of the Malian masses.

Since the 1960s, when oil revenue gave it the means to indulge in disseminating its 'soft' power, Saudi Arabia has been busy exporting Abd al-Wahab's ultra-conservative doctrines to the furthest corners of the Muslim world, through the funding of religious education, mosques and satellite TV channels. The notion that saint-worship is sinful has travelled with those doctrines.

In Afghanistan and Pakistan, the Taliban and their Salafi allies have been attacking Sufi shrines for a decade or more. In 2010 a suicide bomber killed 42 people in the shrine of the saint Hazrat Data Ganj Bakhsh Ali Hujweri in Lahore, also known as the Data Darbar, one of the most revered and ancient sites of Sufi pilgrimage in southern Asia. In April 2011 two suicide bombers killed another 40 pilgrims during a major Sufi festival in the Pakistani Punjab. This destruction has provoked a spirited backlash from more moderate Sufi Muslims in Pakistan, especially those belonging to the generally peaceful Barelvi movement. In 2001, The Taliban also famously destroyed the massive ancient Buddhas of Bamiyan, one of the wonders of Asia. According to Mullah Omar, the Taliban leader, they were "shrines of unbelievers" and deserved to be obliterated.

In 2012, Libyan Wahabis or *Najdis*, as they're sometimes called, bulldozed the shrine of the Sufi saint as-Sha'ab al-Dahmani in Tripoli and the tomb of the 15th century scholar Abdel Salam al-Asmar in Zlitan, where they also set fire to a library full of ancient manuscripts. In Benghazi, they ransacked an ancient burial ground and removed the remains of 30 venerated Muslim sages. They also vandalised the Second World War tombs of allied soldiers near the city. As we'll see, Wahabi iconoclasm isn't always restricted to religious monuments or tombs, but is also sometimes visited on symbols of secular importance.

In Yemen, as far back as 1994, the mausoleum of Sayyid Abu Bakr Al Aydarus, a 15th century Sufi scholar and poet who is considered to be the patron saint of Aden, was pulverised by RPGs and bulldozers. More recently, fighters belonging to Al Qaida in the Arabian Peninsula have ransacked the ancient shrine of al-Ja'dani in at-Tareyah and demolished tombs in Jaar and other towns.

Soon after the overthrow of President Hosni Mubarak in Egypt, Salafis started to target mosques and shrines revered by the country's Sufi orders. In the town of Qalyoub, in the dead of night, a group of extremists attacked the mausoleum of Sidi Abdel Rahman. Five of Qalyoub's other tombs were also destroyed. The city of Alexandria, a historic centre for Egyptian Sufism, became a focal point for Salafi vandalism. Egypt's new moderate Islamist President Mohammed Morsi has even been urged by Salafi ultras in his own country and the Middle East to destroy the most famous "symbols of paganism" on the planet; the Pyramids of Giza. Their destruction has been devoutly desired by ultra-orthodox clerics since the first Muslim invasion of Egypt in the 7th century, but until now the technology to carry out what would surely be the ultimate act of vandalism, has not been readily available.

It is clear that Mali is a sub-plot in a much broader cultural struggle that is raging through the Muslim world. It is a battle for the heart of the Muslim faith, as crucial to the future of Islam as the religious wars of the 15th and 16th centuries between Catholics and Protestants were to the subsequent development of Christianity. Perhaps it's foolish to make direct comparisons between the destruction of countless frescos, carvings, paintings and other priceless art by the followers of Cromwell, Calvin and Zwingli during the Protestant reformation and the wrecking of shrines, tombs and manuscripts in the Muslim world by followers of Abd al-Wahab. Different religion; different doctrines; different time. But in broad philosophical and emotional terms, the Protestant storm against saints and graven images sends a powerful echo back through history.

The Protestant reformers believed that man needed no intermediaries such as saints, priests, bishops or kings to know God. They also considered the old hierarchy of the church and the state to be irreparably corrupt and ungodly, just as Wahabi hotheads today decry the corruption of both secular leaders in the Muslim world and the senior hierarchy of the main Sufi orders, whom they also accuse of spiritual arrogance and exploitation. For the Puritans and Calvinists of the 16th and 17th centuries, the presence of paintings, music, carvings and tapestries in places of worship was a sensual distraction that seduced worshipers away from the simple unadorned divinity of God. Their iconoclastic rampages left ordinary Christian men and women forlorn, robbed of the spiritual landscape they had become accustomed to since birth. In Holland they called it a *beeldenstorm*; a storm of image destruction.

In 1528, the great savant and philosopher of the northern European renaissance, Erasmus, watched that storm hit the town of Basle in Switzerland. "Not a statue has been left," he wrote afterwards in a letter to a friend, "in the churches or in the monasteries; all the frescoes have been whitewashed over. Everything which would burn has been set on fire, everything else hacked into little pieces. Neither value nor artistry prevailed to save anything."

14. Words of God, holy things and beautiful tales

The significance of Timbuktu

"Salt comes from the north, and gold from the south,
Silver comes from the land of the white people,
But the words of God, the holy things, the beautiful tales,
Can only be found in Timbuktu."

- An old proverb, sometimes attributed to
Ahmed Baba al-Massufi al-Timbukti

When the world learned that the MNLA had seized control of Timbuktu on April 1st 2012, it wasn't clear at first that an Islamist takeover of the city was imminent. Press reports gave the impression that although Iyad Ag Ghali and his Islamist Ansar ud-Dine militia had helped the MNLA to defeat the Malian army, this was a victory for Touareg nationalism first and foremost, not for Islam and shari'a law.

Almost as soon as Timbuktu fell however, the alliance between the MNLA and the Islamist Ansar ud-Dine, which had always been founded on convenience rather than belief, began to unravel. On April 2nd, Agence France Presse announced that the three senior emirs of the Saharan branch of Al Qaida in the Islamic Maghreb – Abdelhamid Abou Zeid, Mokhtar Belmokhtar and Yahya Abou al-Hamam – had been sighted in Timbuktu. After more than a decade of kidnapping, racketeering and clandestine holy war, these battle-scarred sons of Algeria's brutal civil conflict had crawled out from hiding to take control of the one of the most famous cities in Africa.

For the next few months, Ansar ud-Dine / AQIM and the MNLA controlled the city in a state of uneasy cohabitation, eyeing each other suspiciously as they roamed about in their 4x4s garlanded with either the green, red, black and gold flag of Azawad, or the black flag of the Salafiya. The MNLA were quartered at the airport south of the city centre and controlled the all-important ferry crossing over the Niger. AQIM and Ansar ud-Dine controlled the city centre.

Towards the end of June, after losing control of Gao, the nominal 'capital' of Azawad, to MUJAO, the MNLA withdrew from all the main cities of Azawad, broke and depleted. Timbuktu fell under the complete control of the Islamist coalition. Abou Zeid had already taken up residence in the palatial quarters that Colonel Khadafy had built in 2005 for his grand 'audience' with the great and the good of the Sahel. A merciless form of 'monkey' Shari'a law was imposed on the population from early April onwards, complete with frequent whippings and dismemberments. Timbuktu became, in effect, the first Al Qaida run city-state in the world. For those implacable 'Ikhwan' in AQIM, embittered by the countless 'humiliations' that their faith had suffered over the centuries at the hands of apostate Christians and corrupt ungodly Muslims, the ancient city of Timbuktu was a holy prize indeed.

Why is Timbuktu so important? Why is this sand blown market town near the shores of the great Niger River so famous throughout the world? Why does its name resonate so deeply in the European imagination? Why does it hold such an important place in the annals of African Islam?

By the time the traveller Leo Africanus visited the town and wrote about it in his book *The History and Description of Africa and of the Notable Things Therein Contained*, first published in Italian in 1591, Timbuktu had evolved from a tiny village favoured by local nomads as a place to water animals into a major 'port' on the southern 'shore' of the great Sahara desert. It was an equally major port on the northern shore of the great Niger River. In other words, as the saying goes, it was "the place where the camel meets the canoe." Timbuktu wasn't the only important caravan stop in the Sahel. Cities like es-Souk to the east or Walata and Awadaghost to the west preceded Timbuktu as trading centres, funnelling the wealth of the Mediterranean down into the *Bilád as Sudan*, the 'Land of the Blacks', and the wealth of Africa – gold, ivory, salt, slaves, ostrich feathers and more – back up to North Africa, Europe and the Middle East.

Mansa Musa 1st, the 'King of Kings' and ruler of the Malian Empire, who was recently accorded the title of the richest man in the history of mankind by the British daily paper The Independent, took possession of Timbuktu on his way back from a pilgrimage to Mecca in 1324. It was during that pilgrimage, with its legendary stopovers in Cairo and Damascus, that Mansa Musa's boundless largesse caused dramatic inflation in the European gold market. In Timbuktu, he commissioned the Andalusian diplomat and administrator Abou al-Haq es-Saheli, whom he had met in Mecca, to build the great mosque of Djinguereber, which was completed in 1330. By the late Middle Ages, Timbuktu was eclipsing rival caravan ports like Djenné and Gao in terms of volume of trade and cultural importance.

Thanks in large part to the widespread notoriety of King Mansa Musa and his legendary riches, the popularity of Leo Africanus' writings and the increasing trade links between Europe and Africa, Timbuktu became famed throughout Christendom as a fabulously rich emporium on the edge of the known world. In the psycho-geography of northern Europe, Timbuktu became a by-word for remoteness, wealth and mystery. Despite declining importance, it has remained so ever since.

Trade brought knowledge and science to Timbuktu as men of intellect travelled there from North Africa, the Middle East and the other Sahelian cities. The town earned a reputation as an open, secure and welcoming haven for learning. After the fall of the Islamic kingdom of Granada in 1492 and the end of Arab domination of al-Andalus, a handful of precious manuscripts were brought there for safekeeping, joining countless others to form the largest collection of books that sub-Saharan Africa had known until then.

Timbuktu lived its golden years during the reign of the Songhai emperor Askia Mohammed 1st in the early 16th century. The 'universities' of Sankoré, Djinguereber and Sidi Yahya had already become famous throughout the Muslim world and received thousands of students every year.

I write 'universities' in quotation marks, because according to Professor John Hunwick, a leading expert in the Arabic literature of West Africa, the often used designation of 'university' cannot justifiably be applied to Timbuktu, as no such centralised educational establishment existed in the city. In fact, students attended a myriad of medium and small-sized madrassas and home-based teaching facilities.

If Timbuktu couldn't quite rival other Muslim cities like Cairo, Fez and Kairouan as centres of further education and intellectual brilliance, it certainly didn't lag far behind. Its men of learning and religion were revered from the Atlantic to the Dead Sea; men like Ahmed Baba al-Massufi al-Timbukti, Mohammed Bagayogo as-Sudani al-Timbukti or Modibo Mohammed al-Kaburi. Most of them were Sufis belonging to the Qadiri order and adherents of the relatively moderate Maliki school of Islamic jurisprudence. When they died, they were buried in simple adobe mausoleums at strategic points within and around the city, forming a kind of psycho-geographical ring of protection for local people. They became the 333 saints of Timbuktu, who seemed destined to rest eternally at peace, protected by the warm reverence of future generations.

After Ahmed 1st of Morocco, also known as al-Mansour 'The Victorious', sent his mercenary army to take control of Timbuktu and its fabled gold mines in 1591, the city slowly declined in importance. The opening up of trade across the Atlantic and up the coast to Europe robbed the trans-Saharan caravan routes of their exclusivity and power. Timbuktu itself became a trophy in games of power that pitted Moroccans against the declining Songhai Empire or local Touareg tribes and eventually all three against the Massina and Toucouleur Empires. Throughout the seventeenth and eighteenth centuries, the city slowly waned to a ghost of its former self. According to the Frenchman René Caillé, who visited the fabled town in 1828, the first European to do so and return home alive, Timbuktu presented nothing but a drab vista of dirty dusty streets and low-built adobe houses gently baking under the implacable sun.

But the symbol remained alive. The tropes of "Timbuktu the mysterious" and "Timbuktu the remote" were overtaken in the middle of the 20th century by "Timbuktu, cradle of West African learning and science", as African intellectuals both at home and abroad began to re-appropriate and redefine the image of the continent, wresting it free from the oppression of colonial arrogance and disdain. The conviction grew that far from being a 'dark' continent without history, science, religion or learning and thus 'legitimately' open to exploitation and enslavement, Africa had in fact enjoyed an intellectual and spiritual golden age in Timbuktu and other cities of the Sahel such as Walata, Djenné, Katsina, Agadez, Gao and Kano, with institutions of learning that rivalled and even excelled those in both the Christian and Muslim worlds.

This golden intellectual and scientific age in the Sahel became the prime counter-argument to the racist credo of colonialism and slavery elegantly expressed by the 19th century American writer John C Calhoun when he wrote the following about slaves in Deep South: "never before has the black race of Central Africa, from the dawn of history to the present day, attained a condition so civilised and so improved, not only physically, but morally and intellectually."

The claim that Africa never had any civilisation and was in effect 'rescued' by European advancement and enlightenment is still being propounded today, not least by the ex-French president Nicholas Sarkozy. In 2007 he gave a speech in Senegal in which he declared that "The tragedy of Africa is that the African has never really entered into history… The African peasant, who for thousands of years has lived according to the seasons, whose life ideal was to be in harmony with nature, only knew the eternal renewal of time… In this imaginary world, where everything starts over and over again, there is room neither for human endeavour, nor for the idea of progress… The problem of Africa is to be found here. Africa's challenge is to enter to a greater extent into history… It is to realise that the golden age that Africa is forever recalling will not return, because it has never existed."

Sarkozy was wrong. That golden age, that 'entering into history' existed in Timbuktu, in Walata, in the Ghana, Mali and Songhoi Empires and in more recent manifestations of African resistance, from the anti-colonial struggles of Cheikh Amadou Bamba Mbacké or El Hadj Oumar Tall, to the independence movements of the 20th century. Men like Kwame Nkrumah, Patrice Lumumba, Leopold Senghor,

Samora Machel and Nelson Mandela were driven by the idea of progress and the passionate belief that Africa could renew itself through human endeavour. Timbuktu, often referred to as the 'pearl' of the desert, has become one of the most important symbolic pillars of that new African pride. It is not that the dirt brown streets, ramshackle markets or cloistered houses of Timbuktu shine pearly white, but its past, its supreme importance for Africa's self-image and the hope it inspires for Africa's future.

Timbuktu was both an outpost of the Andalusian enlightenment of the Middle Ages and a centre of Islamic study and piety. As such it became a symbol of both faith and tolerance. It was a place where refugees from southern Spain, students from the Middle East, wise men from the Maghreb, sages from south of the Niger could meet and discourse. Those scholars of the Quran, those specialists of the hadīth and Islamic *fiqh* or jurisprudence found their cosmopolitan haven on the banks of the Niger, in black Africa. And like the Cordoba or Granada of the tenth and eleventh centuries, Timbuktu's past proposes a model for a brighter future in which Islam will once again become a conduit for openness, tolerance and fearless enquiry rather than obscurantism or insularity.

That is why the Salafi takeover of Timbuktu in April 2012 presented not only an actual crisis of desperate acuteness for the people of the city, the country and the region but also a symbolic crisis for Africa and Islam.

15. "We have come here to teach you the true faith"

Vandalism and destruction along the great fault line of the Sahel

"We have come here to teach you the true faith," says a tall *mujahid*, or Islamist soldier, to a small gathering of local Timbuktu people. He wears a plain brown *bouboul* – a traditional ankle length robe – and a light sandy coloured *cheche*, the turban worn by men, which covers his entire head, leaving only his eyes visible to the world. An AK47 hangs over his left shoulder, and khaki pouches festoon his belt. His voice is calm, 'reasonable', and his hands accompany his words with elegant gestures.

A local Songhai man gives the camera capturing the scene a bemused, conciliatory smile. He looks neither doubtful nor convinced, just gently puzzled. "*Ouaha*," someone says softly in Arabic, "ok." The mujahid and his fellow fighters continue to smash up old wooden statues of African deities, pounding them into the dusty street of Timbuktu. They're the kind of statues that might have sat in the corner of a local home, like old friends, or formed expectant ranks in the dark interior of some local tourist emporium, waiting to be bought and carried back to Europe as a memento; dusty, mute and alien to foreign eyes.

Then another mujahid brings out a piece of paper, on which a benediction has been written. With it, he holds a little wrap containing a talisman, the kind that thousands and thousands of Malians wear in small leather pouches around their necks as a humble plea to invisible powers for protection and *baraka* – blessings. The mujahid brandishes the paper as if it were proof of some great sin and unwraps the package in front of his audience, which comprises mostly children who can barely hide their puzzled glee at this unexpected diversion from the banality of their daily routine. The mujahid then lights the piece of paper and holds disdainfully between thumb and forefinger while it burns to ash.

Just a piece of paper. Just a little wrap. Just an old statue. Just a mud hut.

The tomb of Sidi Mahmoud Ben Amar Mohammed Ben Aqit, which used to stand to the north of Timbuktu in the cemetery that also bears his name, was certainly no architectural marvel. It was a simple one roomed adobe hut, with old wooden roof joists, semi-ornate doors and windows and a rendering of more modern breezeblocks to protect it from the annual rains. During the saint's lifetime, this modest structure had been part of his home. Around him in the Sidi Mahmoud cemetery lay the tombs of another 167 of Timbuktu's 333 saints.

When mujahedeen claiming to belong to the Touareg militia Ansar ud-Dine, but more likely to be affiliated directly to Al Qaida in the Islamic Maghreb, came to vandalise the tomb on Friday May 4th 2012, there was little danger of the world losing a grand piece of architectural heritage. This wasn't the Taj Mahal or the mausoleum of Tamerlane in Samarkand. But something was most definitely lost, something more powerful to local people than art. It was the peace and repose of a friend, a protector; it was a sense of respect and reverence that made life stable and liveable; it was a place to contemplate, to give thanks, to utter supplications for comfort or good fortune; it was a piece of history of immense worth not only to Timbuktu, but to the whole of Africa and the Muslim world.

It was this symbolic value that the Ansar ud-Dine militiamen objected to. "What you're doing is sinful! Ask God directly, rather than a dead man," they shouted at the mute crowd who had been carrying out their observances at Sidi

Mahmoud's tomb that Friday of prayer. An angry cluster of bystanders gathered to watch as the mujahedeen, led by a Mauritanian man who had just arrived in Timbuktu for the purpose, smashed the door to the mausoleum and ripped down the thin white veils covering the tomb of the saint. Those veils, left by supplicants in the hope that their prayers would be granted, were then burned in full view of the onlookers. One of them tried to protest, but he was bound, gagged and bundled into the boot of a car. It wasn't the first such act of religious iconoclasm in modern Malian history, but it was the first to make a victim of the memory of a saint as great as Sidi Mahmoud and it provoked local grief and international outrage.

In important ways, the scenes of vandalism and destruction that were played out in Timbuktu following the Salafist takeover in April 2012 weren't new at all. There was something very old about them. Mostly white Arabic or Hassaniya speaking men from the northern deserts were 'teaching' the blacks how to worship Allah in the 'proper' manner. Granted, some of the mujahedeen might have been black Africans from the Nigerian Islamist terror group Boko Haram or soldiers of fortune from southern Mali, Burkina Faso, Senegal and Guinea. But the ringleaders and spokespersons were mainly Arab northerners; either local Berabiche from the Timbuktu region, Sahrawis from northern Mauritania and Western Sahara or Algerians from the Touat and Tidikelt. Some of them were Touareg. Just as the Ikhwan of Saudi Arabia unleashed their righteous ire on the people of the Hijaz, the AQIM overlords of Timbuktu were imposing an alien religious philosophy by force of arms on local people with a very different cultural outlook to theirs and, in this case, a different skin colour too. It was a scenario that had been replayed for centuries along the cultural 'fault' line that stretches from Mauritania in the west to the Sudan in the east, separating the 'white' Arab and

Berber people of the north from the 'black' African peoples of the south.

Unsurprisingly, black Malian religious leaders were averse to the idea of being re-educated about Islam whilst men from the north pointed a gun at their heads. Something that characterised many of the local responses to the Salafist occupation of Timbuktu and other parts of northern Mali was the defiant claim that Mali had no need of any lessons from strangers on how to be good Muslims. Mali is proud of its own religious traditions, however innovative and sinful they may seem to the followers of Abd al-Wahab.

After the Islamist takeover there was a constant war of words between the leaders of AQIM, MUJAO and Ansar ud-Dine and the religious hierarchy in the larger northern towns. Points of religious law were debated with the imams of the great mosques, often on absurdly abstruse grounds of contention. A fine example occurred when the Islamist occupiers entered the Djinguereber Mosque in Timbuktu to try and prevent the Grand Imam from using a microphone and loud speakers during prayers. For the Salafis, the use of such a modern technology was anathema simply because it didn't exist in the time of The Prophet. The imam of Djinguereber turned the argument on its head and asked the assailants to produce the verse from the Quran that specifically forbids the use of microphones and speakers during prayers. The Islamists had no answer and grudgingly left.

"Everything they do is contrary to the principles of Islam," was the sweeping rebuff expressed by Alphadi Wangara, the imam of Sidi Yahya mosque in Timbuktu, in an interview for the Malian newspaper *22 Septembre*. "That's been obvious from day one. At the first meeting they held with all the imams of the city, they wanted us to believe that they had to come to move Islam forward in Timbuktu. We've subsequently learned what their word is worth… We met them and made it clear that we know the principles of Islam. The Prophet Mohammed, peace be upon his name, explained the word of God to men using his wisdom. We pointed out to them that the very fact they're trampling our soil, forcing their way into places of worship and roaming around town with their weapons in their hands is forbidden under Islam. All good Muslims know that in order to impose shari'a law, one must be righteous oneself. Whereas these Islamists are far from being righteous men." The fact is however, that imam Wangara gave this interview in Bamako. In order to speak his mind without fear, he had been forced to leave his home and go into exile. The pride and defiance of Mali's traditional religious leaders meant little in the face of whips and AK47s.

It wasn't just religious building or symbols that were subjected to the Salafist ire. It was also symbols of an entirely secular, democratic and republican nature. On April 25th 2012, a week before the desecration of the mausoleum of Sidi Mahmoud Ben Amar, the Islamists decapitated the statue of Al Farouk, the mythical horseman and protector of Timbuktu, which dominated Place de l'Indépendence in central Timbuktu. The monument had been erected in 1960 to celebrate the independence of Mali and local legend had it that the turbaned horse-rider would descend from his perch at night and roam the streets of the city, keeping citizens safe from harm.

"I smashed the al-Farouk monument with my own hands because local people told me that he was the spirit protector of the town," a militiaman called Mohammed Kasse, aka Abou Zaar, told TV5. "I broke it to prove to them that he means nothing and that only God can protect us." The Islamists also destroyed the mausoleum of Cheikh Mohammed Tamba Tamba, an early 19th century scholar from the maraboutic Touareg tribe known as the Kel es-Souk. The tomb was situated within the perimeter fence of

Fort Cheick Sidi Bakaye, the military barracks next to Place de l'Indépendence that had been taken over by AQIM in early April 2012. It seemed that the presence of a dead saint in their midst was too much for the mujahedeen to bear. Four months later, on October 30th, another group of militiamen bulldozered what remained of the Al Farouk monument, including the headless horseman, his horse and the inelegant early 1960s V-shaped plinth on which they rode. Timbuktu's mythical protector was gone.

On May 16th, the Islamists destroyed the Monument of the Martyrs in Timbuktu. It had been erected in homage to the young students and protestors who had helped to overthrow the hated Malian dictator Moussa Traore in March 1991.

"They tried to smash the monument with tools, and it didn't work," a teacher told Jeune Afrique. "Then they tied a rope around the monument, which was attached to a vehicle. It drove slowly away and brought the monument down." Almost every city or town in Mali has its *Monument des Martyrs*. They commemorate an event of which every Malian can feel proud; a moment of national rage and courage that brought democracy in its wake. That is the tragic circularity in the Malian narrative. The nation shed its blood to bring in democracy. That democracy was then used and abused by a corrupt and self-serving political elite who allowed their country to fall into the hands of *les fous de Dieu…* God's crazy ones. As a result, the country split in two and this in turn precipitated a military coup that killed off democracy. Back to square one.

Why destroy a monument dedicated to young defenceless Malian patriots who sacrificed their blood to overthrow a military dictator? Did the mujahedeen deem even this anodyne tribute to people power to be a distraction from the One God? Many perceived a more sinister strategy behind Al Qaida's vandalism. They were purposefully destroying symbols and spiritual objects that gave meaning to people's lives in the hope of breaking their resistance and controlling them more easily. Amadou O., an inhabitant of Timbuktu who once worked in the decimated tourism sector, told the news channel France 24 that it was difficult to put up any resistance against the invader. "Local people are wounded to the bone by what's happening," he said, "and they've completely lost their bearings for the moment." The French word he used was *déboussolé*, which literally means 'de-compassed'. Losing familiar landmarks in their spiritual landscape deprived Timbuktu's inhabitants of their compass.

The Bamako-based rapper and social activist Amkoullel gives his own explanation of 'de-compassing'. "The aim of those Islamists is to destroy all reference, all memory and history," he says. "That's why they attack the mausoleums. That's why they destroy culture and music. Because when you destroy all the reference of a people, its memory, which is preserved in its museums, its monuments, its music and culture, well, then it's like they don't have a past any more, and you can replace it with what you're proposing. That's the first stage of alienation."

The tomb-storm

What had started as a trickle in late April and early May became a flood in late June. On the last day of that month, a Saturday, the Islamists went on an iconoclastic rampage, damaging or completely destroying seven of the sixteen most prestigious tombs around the city. They began their spree by returning to the mausoleum of Sidi Mahmoud in north of the city and reducing it to a pile of rubble with hoes, spades and pick-axes. Then they moved to the east of the city and attacked the tomb of Cheikh Alpha Moya Idjé Tjina Sare, a pious savant who was assassinated in front of the Sankoré mosque with fifteen other saints by the Moroccan Pasha Mohamed Ben Zarquoun in 1594.

The tomb-storm headed towards the northeastern corner of the town and the tomb of Cheikh Sidi el-Mokhtar Ben Sidi Mohammed Ben Cheikh al-Kebir al-Kounti, a renowned philosopher who died in 1811. Cheikh el-Mokhtar's grandson, Cheikh Ahmed al-Bekkay al-Kounti, befriended the German explorer Heinrich Barth, who spent seven months in Timbuktu in 1853 to 1854. He was, according to Barth, a man of considerable learning and wisdom.

Cheikh al-Bekkay wrote a famous letter to Ahmadou Lobbo, emir of the Fulani Kingdom of Hamdallahi, who had been fighting a jihad to restore the true Islamic faith and impose strict shari'a law in the Massina region and especially the cities of Segou and Timbuktu. The letter defended Cheikh al-Bekkay's right to receive Barth in Timbuktu, a town that was officially off-limits to Christians and unbelievers. In it he writes "I never thought that a man like you could have no knowledge of the rules to which jihad must be subjected…that it is forbidden to be unjust against an infidel whoever he may be, fighter or non-fighter, who has entered the lands of Islam with a safe-conduct given to him by a Muslim."

Cheikh Ahmed al-Bekkay was the grand master of the Qadiriyya Sufi brotherhood in the Sahara, and the chief of a powerful Arab tribe known as the Kounta. The destruction of his grandfather's tomb by AQIM and Ansar ud-Dine on June 30th 2012 rings with multiple historical ironies. It was a blow against the tradition of tolerance and peace propounded in Cheikh Ahmed's famous letter to his Fulani overlord. It was yet another strike against the Sufi traditions of West Africa. It was also an act of class warfare. Being the dominant temporal and religious 'nobility' of the northern Arabs of Mali, the Kounta had long been resented by 'lower' class Berabiche Arabs, who dominate trans-Saharan trading and smuggling. AQIM has strong allies, even marriage ties, with the Berabiche of Timbuktu. The destruction of the mausoleum of such an important Kounta ancestor was, in part, a declaration of defiance and contempt on the part of the Berabiche Arabs who wielded the pickaxes.

Even the venerable Djinguereber mosque was not spared from the Salafist fury. On July 1st, a group of mujahedeen with hoes and pickaxes destroyed three mausoleums adjacent to the western wall of the mosque, the thud of their strikes mingling with their cries of "*Allah u-Akbar! Allah u-Akbar!*" ("God is Great!"). A film crew from Al Jazeera was invited to film the destruction. The roads leading to the mosque were blocked but when the Ansar ud-Dine fighters saw people gathering to witness the destruction they fired shots over their heads. The tombs belonged to three saints; Sidi Elmety, Mahamane Elmety and Cheick Sidi Amar. Over half of the most important mausoleums in Timbuktu now lay in ruins.

On July 2nd, Ansar ud-Dine and AQIM descended on the Sidi Yahya mosque, ripping off the famous door that had remained shut for more than three centuries, and desecrating the tomb of the saint inside the mosque. Sidi Yahya al Tadilsi was one of the savants who brought Sufism to Timbuktu at the end of the 15th century. His blessings were sought by pilgrims and supplicants centuries after his death; for health, good fortune, rain, a happy marriage, security and spiritual guidance. This was all apostasy to the Salafi leaders of Ansar ud-Dine and Al Qaida.

There was another dimension to all this iconoclasm that derived from a deep hatred of the West. In the weeks preceding the tomb-storm in Timbuktu, Mrs Lalla Ben Barka, UNESCO's under-Director for Africa, had been in Bamako for emergency meetings with the Malian Ministry of Culture and other bodies to discuss the destruction of the tomb of Sidi Mahmoud and the Al-Farouk monument. At the end of her stay Mrs Ben Barka gave a press conference and reminded her audience that Mali was a signatory to

UNESCO's Convention Concerning the Protection of the World Cultural and Natural Heritage (1972) and that Mali's heritage sites should be protected under the terms of the Convention.

On June 28th, at the request of the Malian government, the World Heritage Committee of UNESCO placed Timbuktu and the Tomb of Emperor Mohammed Askia 1st in Gao on the UNESCO List of World Heritage in Danger. This move followed repeated expressions of concern from Irina Bokova, director general of UNESCO, who requested that the armed groups in Mali protect the built heritage and precious objects in Timbuktu. The city itself had been granted UNESCO World Heritage status in 1988.

UNESCO's entreaties only served to exacerbate the fury of Timbuktu's Islamist occupiers. A heavily bearded young spokesperson for Ansar ud-Dine called Sanda Ould Bounama claimed that the Islamist tomb-storm of the weekend of June 30th 2012 was a direct retaliation against UNESCO's meddling in the affairs of Islam. "Ansar ud-Dine will destroy every mausoleum in the city," he told AFP, "All of them, without exception. God is unique. All of this is *haram*. We are all Muslims. UNESCO is what?" That turn of phrase – *"UNESCO c'est quoi?"* – is often used in Francophone Africa to express a particularly disdainful form of contempt. Ould Bounama was effectively saying that UNESCO meant nothing to him and that UN jurisdiction was not recognised in the territory under their control.

Cheikh Ag Aoussa, the right hand man and genuine mouthpiece of the Ansar ud-Dine leader Iyad Ag Ghaly, told the press that "it isn't for the West to say what is holy and what isn't. We ask them not to meddle in our culture and our Islam." Another of Ansar ud-Dine's bewildering array of mostly self-appointed spokespersons, this time a Tunisian by the name of Ahmed, also told AFP that from now on, whenever foreigners spoke about Timbuktu, the armed group would attack anything referred to as a site of World Heritage. "There is no world heritage," he declared. "It doesn't exist. The infidels must not get involved in our business."

There was also a feeling among the jihadists that UNESCO was demonstrating a typically Western and hypocritical concern for culture and art, when human beings were suffering in the Sahel. Ironically, this view is also shared by Fadimata Walet Oumar aka 'Disco', founder and leader of the Touareg group Tartit, an outspoken woman who is otherwise viscerally opposed to the Islamist occupation of her homeland. "For me, a mausoleum is a building, a tomb," she tells me over the phone from a refugee camp in Burkina Faso. "If it is destroyed you can always rebuild it. But you can't bring back people's lives. You can't give back dignity to the people who've been forced into refugee camps. Abroad they're always talking about the mausoleums in Timbuktu, but they're not talking enough about all those children, those women who have been thrown out of their country. For me, personally, a tomb is a tomb. But the dignity of a people who have been humiliated by exodus, by the fact that we're in a country we don't belong to and we have to queue up in front of the HCR post every day with our bowls, that's worse that the destruction of the biggest mausoleum on earth."

Disco is at odds with international opinion. The Chief Prosecutor of the International Criminal Court in the Hague, Mrs Fatou Bensaouda, told AFP on July 1st that the destruction of tombs and heritage was a war crime which her office had full authority to investigate. "My message to those involved in these criminal acts is clear: stop the destruction of religious buildings now." Mrs Bensaouda cited the Rome Statute that established the ICC and to which Mali is a signatory. Article 8 states that a deliberate attack against an undefended civilian building that is not a military objective is a war crime. "This includes attacks against historical monuments as well as destruction of building dedicated to religion," she said.

The shock caused by the tomb-storm in Timbuktu was also deeply felt within Mali. Thousands of people took to the streets of Bamako on July 4th to protest against the destruction of the country's heritage. They were led by the South's most powerful religious leaders, including Mahmoud Dicko, the President of the High Islamic Council. The present day spiritual leader of the Kounta Arabs, Cheikh Alpha Dahar Kounta, also took part.

Meanwhile, in the north, vigilante groups were formed to protect other important mausoleums and buildings. In Gao, a group of young Songhai men mounted guard over the 16th century tomb of the great Emperor Mohammed Askia 1st, the ruler of the Songhai Empire, one of the greatest polities that West Africa has ever known. North of Timbuktu, an Arab militia that called itself the Tahel Ould Sidi brigade was formed to defend the mausoleums in the towns of Araouane and Gasser Cheikh. They were especially keen to protect the tomb of Cheikh Sidi Ahmed Ag Adda, a religious leader of great piety and learning who came from the town of es-Souk to establish Araouane in the 17th century and made it an intellectual and religious centre of some renown.

"We won't allow people who don't know their Islam to come and destroy our treasures," declared one of the brigade leaders. "I have studied in Mauritania and Saudi Arabia and no one tells us in the Holy Quran that we should destroy tombs." Following the Ansar ud-Dine threat to destroy mausoleums not only in Timbuktu itself but also in the entire Timbuktu region, a convoy of 4x4 vehicles full of militiamen was despatched north on July 6th to raze the tomb of Cheikh ag Adda and others in the Araouane area. On the way, the convoy suffered a severe car crash that left four Ansar ud-Dine fighters dead and another twelve injured.

Divine intervention or a simple twist of fate, the tomb of the great saint was spared.

The destruction didn't stop in July. On September 15th, radicals from the MUJAO Islamist group who control Gao destroyed the tomb of a great Kounta savant called Cheikh El Kebir, the 'Great Cheikh', which was situated about 300 kilometres north of the town. A few weeks later, towards the end of September, the tombs of Almirou Mahamane Assidiki and Alfa Mobo were wrecked in Goundam, an important town about 100 kilometres south-west of Timbuktu. "It wounded my heart," an inhabitant of Goundam told the French radio station RFI. "But if that's the straight path I think I can only submit and ask pardon of God, that's all. They're the masters of this place and one can only submit to their wishes. According what I hear from various people, there's some truth in what they say." The Islamists filmed the destruction for posterity.

In October, Ansar ud-Dine made their mark on the newly occupied town of Douentza, an important truck stop between Timbuktu and Mopti inhabited mainly by Fulani people. The town became the southern frontline of the Islamist advance southwards in early September 2012, too close for the comfort of most southern Malians, especially those living in Mopti, Mali's second biggest city. On Monday 8th October, the mujahedeen tied a chain to the pillars of the *Toguna*, or meetinghouse of the male elders in the town, and tore it apart with their Toyota Land Cruisers.

The Toguna is a traditional Dogon structure that consists of a series of carved pillars and adobe walls surmounted by a platform and a thick thatch roof made out of millet stalks. It is a place for men to parlay and resolve conflicts. They say that the roof of a Toguna is built deliberately low so that no one can stand up and commit an act of violence under it. The walls of the Toguna are often decorated with animals and geometric motifs of mystical origin. The Salafist militiamen who took control of Douentza disapproved of such 'idolatrous' imagery and its old Toguna, one of the finest in southern Mali, was destroyed.

On October 18th the tomb-storm returned to Timbuktu, as militiamen started to destroy mausoleums in Kabara, the suburb 12 kilometres south of the city which serves as its port on the Niger River. They also finished off the Al Farouk monument. The UNESCO director general Irina Bokova issued another condemnation to the general indifference of the mujahedeen.

On December 23rd 2012, the mujahedeen in the city implemented the last phase of the 'moral cleansing' that had begun back in May. Teams were sent out to destroy all Timbuktu's remaining tombs. "Not a single mausoleum will be left," yet another Ansar ud-Dine spokesperson, this time with the jihadi nickname of Abou Dardar, told AFP. "God doesn't like this. We're destroying all the tombs hidden in the various neighbourhoods." A local inhabitant contacted by phone confirmed the tomb-storm. "I saw the Islamists get out of their vehicle near Timbuktu's main mosque," said one. "Behind a house they destroyed a tomb crying *God is great, God is great!*"

These final acts of destruction targeted the many smaller tombs that were hidden away in the narrow alleyways of Timbuktu's old town. The timing was significant. On December 20th, the UN Security Council passed resolution 2085 authorising the use of force to recapture northern Mali and make the country whole again. Once again, by taking their pick-axes to the cultural heritage so cherished by the wider world, Al Qaida was demonstrating its defiance of Western *kuffar* 'meddling'.

French paratroopers floated down onto Timbuktu's airport on January 28th 2013, a 'heavenly visitation' that was greeted by the city's battered population with unrestrained dancing, singing and shouts of "Vive Hollande! Vive la France! Vive le Mali!"

The relief was overwhelming. All around lay small heaps of rubble, the sorry vestiges of Timbuktu's spiritual heritage. On January 30th, UNESCO announced that they would be sending a mission to "undertake a complete evaluation of the damage and determine the most urgent needs, in order to finalise a plan of action…" The tombs will be rebuilt. The task poses no great architectural challenge. The simplicity of these structures was, in some ways, one of their blessings.

When it came to another of Timbuktu's treasures however, the news didn't sound so promising. A day after the French recapture of Timbuktu, the shocked and baleful mayor of Timbuktu, Hallé Ousmane Cissé, called a close contact in the UK to inform her that the departing Islamists had set fire to one of Timbuktu's main libraries and its priceless collection of manuscripts. If Abou Zeid had wanted to outrage the 'Western' sensibility to it very core, he could hardly have chosen a better way to do it.

16. "The knowledge they hold is inestimable"

Historic manuscripts and Africa's memory

What is Mali's most precious cultural asset? In the spiritual, non-material category, the debate around that question could go on for hours, days, even months. Is it music? Or the oral history of the griots? Or the dances of the Donso hunters? Or an Islam deeply rooted in the beliefs of a pre-Islamic age? Or the humour-laden inter-ethnic teasing known as *sinankunya* in the local Bamana language or *cousinage* in French; a kind of rib-tickling mickey-taking and humor that oils ethnic tolerance? Or the traditions of good governance and social fairness handed down since the earliest days of the Manding Empire? The list of candidates is long, and all of them are interconnected.

In the material sphere, the choice is simpler perhaps. Some might claim that the great adobe mosques and mausoleums of Timbuktu, Djenné, Mopti, Gao and the smaller mud mosques that are the pride of hundreds of little towns and villages in the north, should take first prize. Some might propose niche phenomena like Mali's wonderful *bogolan* blankets, the silver jewellery of the Touareg, the gold or beaded jewellery of the Fulani and the Songhai, the wonderful carved doors and statues of the Dogon or even entire Dogon villages, with their sculpted beauty, unique stilted granaries and Toguna meeting places. Mali is a highly cultured place, so the choice is wide. But there's one material treasure that must surely rank amongst the most precious, possibly higher than all the others: Mali's ancient books and manuscripts.

I refer to piles of books, shelf upon buckling shelf of manuscripts, chests stuffed with parchments, boxes overflowing with scrolls and paper, shabby trunks gorged with rotting leather bound volumes, dusty store-rooms full of teetering tomes stacked like mini high-rise dwellings of the most decrepit kind, teeming with their populations of termites, book worms and dust.

In a country blessed with wealth and a fussy appreciation of the importance of culture and heritage, all that old paper would be jealously guarded in air-conditioned vaults and cared for by fastidious men and women wearing white gloves, possibly even hair-nets. Access would be open to all, especially bona fide academics and researchers. Substantial parts of the collection would probably be digitised and consultable online. Every now and then a few choice volumes would be hauled out of the vaults and inserted into a sumptuous public exhibition, with mysteriously lit cabinets, eye-catching blow ups, illustrated panels and fulsome explanations of the wonders contained in the texts themselves.

In Mali, the greatest collection of books and manuscripts in sub-Saharan Africa lies, for the most part, in old wooden chests and metal trunks, or hidden away in storerooms, caves and holes in the sand, providing sustenance for an interesting fauna of insects and microbes. Apart from the fortunate few that were, until recently, carefully archived in well-funded libraries, most of these treasures are dispersed around private homes in Timbuktu, Djenné, Gao, Arouane, Bourem, Bamba, Gourma and other villages on the Niger bend, or in nomadic camps far out in the desert between the great river and the borders with Mauritania, Algeria and Niger. No one knows exactly how many works are out there. Estimates vary between 180,000 and 800,000 all told when you take into account everything from books to manuscripts, letters, parchments, scrolls and unbound, unsorted stacks of paper.

That's not to say that Malians don't care about these treasures or that substantial efforts haven't already been made to save them. In fact, part of the problem is that many of the private manuscript owners care too much. They're often reluctant to allow their family heirlooms be taken away by one of the more professionally run libraries or research institutes in Timbuktu for restoration and preservation. They're fearful that the books will be stolen, lost, or that the simple act of dispersing them will rob their family of the blessings or *baraka* that these venerable old objects are believed to bestow.

An engaging film by the German film-maker Lutz Gregor called *Tombouctou – Les Manuscrits sauvés des sables* follows the quest of Abdel Kader Haidara, a large imposing man born and bred in Timbuktu, to save manuscripts for posterity. Abdel Kader's father Cheikh Mamma Haidara was an intellectual who, like his forebears going back generations, read Arabic. He bought as many books as he could and amassed a collection of 9,000 tomes before he died, often copying them for his own personal use or for teaching purposes. Among them was a 13th century Quran, written on vellum made from the skin of a gazelle.

Haidara father and son both worked at the Ahmed Baba Institute of Higher Learning and Islamic Research, aka IHERI-AB, now the largest library and preservation centre in Timbuktu. It was founded by the Malian state with the help of UNESCO and donations from Kuwait and Saudi Arabia in 1972 and is now home to over 30,000 manuscripts. Until the Islamist takeover of April 2012, a staff of over 20 archivists, restorers, researchers and administrators worked at the brand new institute building, a state of the art archival facility heavily funded by the government of South Africa. The South African president Thabo Mbeki paid an official visit to the town in 2001 and apparently took a personal interest in Timbuktu and its glorious intellectual heyday.

Funding also came from Libya and the late dictator Colonel Muammar Khadafy, who poured money into Timbuktu following the extraordinary pomp and circumstance of his official visit to the city in 2005. Thus money from the Middle East, North Africa and sub-Saharan Africa has been funding the preservation of Timbuktu's history, which is a neat illustration of Timbuktu's pivotal position between the Muslim and African worlds. During their years in power, both Khadafy and Mbeki saw themselves as the guiding lights of a new African century. They considered Timbuktu, its mosques, mausoleums and manuscripts, to be the supreme symbol of what Africa had achieved before the continent was subjugated by trans-Atlantic slavery and colonialism. The city became a weapon in the armoury of their anti-colonial anti-dependency disçourse.

That cusp between the Muslim and the Black African worlds was personified by Ahmed Baba al-Massufi al-Timbukti, the great 16th century scholar, judge, author and political activist, after whom the Institute is named. Professor John Hunwick, a globally renowned authority on West Africa's medieval manuscripts, referred to Ahmed Baba as "only a single, albeit an outstanding example of a tradition of scholarship and teaching in the Western Sudan which went back at least two centuries before his time and continued to flourish after his time and, indeed, still flourishes today." In other words, Ahmed Baba was a man of learning among many, even though the breadth of his scholarship, the number of books attributed to him and his dramatic exile to Morocco at the end of the 16th century have attached a particularly reverent aura to his name. One of his many titles was 'as-Sudani', 'the Black', and he remains the epitome of the African intellectual luminary.

Cheikh Mamma Haidara died in 1981 and his son Abdel Kader became the main 'prospector' for the Ahmed Baba Institute. His job was to journey out to small villages and nomad camps to try and persuade families to part with their precious bibliographic inheritance. It was no easy task. Quite apart from their financial value, the books represented a tangible link with family history. In some ways, they were akin to the fetishes used in ancestor-worship, revered for the sense of solidity, continuity and belonging that they embodied as well as the immense knowledge that they transported from generation to generation.

Family heads and village elders were reluctant to hand these heirlooms over to strangers, distrusting their motives, fearing that their treasures might be stolen or simply lost. Moreover, the books sometimes contained family histories of a very private nature. The scribes who wrote them would often jot down commentaries, bits of local news, rumour and gossip in the margins of erudite texts and they included revelations that are deemed still potent enough to damage a family's reputation to this day. Mixed in amongst the spiritual or academic texts in a collection there are often family papers, accounts, bills of sale, contracts, personal diaries and letters. These documents, whose very banality makes them all the more fascinating to modern historians and researchers, can be very revealing. A distant ancestor could prove to be the illegitimate offspring of a slave, for example, or a grand Timbuktu family, proud of their Islamic piety, might prove to be descended from Andalusian Jews.

Abdel Kader often paid large sums of money for individual works or even entire collections. He also came to learn that owners could sometimes be persuaded to part with their books for a set of good healthy young breeding camels or cattle. "I sold a lot of cows," Abdel Kader told the journalist Joshua Hammer of the Smithsonian magazine. In one village alone he found 2,000 manuscripts. In another, the village chief demanded a new mosque in return for his collection of books, and, after the mosque was built, added a new house and the refurbishment of the village's Quranic school to his sale price for good measure.

The manuscripts sought by Abdel Kader Haidara lay scattered far and wide across northern Mali. This was due to the fact that, in times of conflict, owners would disperse and hide their collections to keep them safe. As Timbuktu declined following the overthrow of the Songhoi Empire by Moroccan troops at the end of the 16th century, dispersal was one of the surest methods of keeping collections out of the covetous hands of successive Touareg, Fulani, Massina and French occupiers. More recently, during the great Touareg uprising of 1990-1991, books and manuscripts were once again hidden away for safekeeping, making their retrieval infinitely harder. In the end, it took Abdel Kader 16 years to acquire more than 16,000 works for the Ahmed Baba Institute, a remarkable feat given the circumstances.

In 1993, Abdel Kader left the institute to take on the challenge of reviving his family's own library. Ironically, family covenants forbade him from selling any of the family manuscripts and so he decided to create a proper home for them in situ, with one branch in Timbuktu and another smaller one in the ancestral village of Bamba, halfway between Timbuktu and Gao. The collection already numbered around 6,000 volumes, the patient accumulation of generations upon generations of learned men, imams, *cadis* – Islamic judges – and teachers, to which Abdel Kader's father had added other volumes purchased in Egypt and Sudan. In the past two decades Abdel Kader has increased the size of the collection to more than 9,000 tomes.

Funds to support Abdel Kader's work were at best meagre, at worst non-existent, but in 1997 help arrived in the shape of the famous Harvard historian Professor Henry Louis Gates Junior, who visited the Haidara collection and was moved to start an appeal. Money donated by the Andrew Mellon Foundation funded a new purpose-built archive in

Timbuktu and the Mamma Haidara Memorial Library was officially opened in the year 2000. Meanwhile, pursuing an initiative that he had launched whilst working at the Institute Baba Ahmed, Abdel Kader set up an association of manuscript owners called *SAVAMA – SAuvegarde et VAlorisation des MAnuscrits* (Preservation and Recovery of Manuscripts). The purpose of the association is to train manuscript owners in preservation and archiving techniques so that they can care for their family collections themselves whilst respecting family traditions and covenants.

With a large grant from the Ford Foundation, SAVAMA helped to build libraries for the al Wangari and Ben Essayouti families. The grant also paid for computers and scanners so that the immense task of digitising the manuscripts could gather pace. Meanwhile, the University of Cape Town and the Ford Foundation set up the Timbuktu Manuscript project, to help train restorers and archivists. The Library of Congress, Lyon's École Normale Supérieure, France's Bibilothèque Nationale, the British Library, the Duchy of Luxemburg and the Juma Al Majid Centre in Dubai have also funded manuscript preservation in Mali.

Teaching families how to look after their own libraries was an important strategic shift in the struggle to safeguard Timbuktu's priceless heritage. Each family collection has its own history and focus. Lamikanati Maygala studied conservation at the Haidara Library in order to care properly for books he inherited from his father, which are stored in a modest two-roomed building in Timbuktu called the al-Mustapha Kounati Badindi Library. The first room is fairly well ordered with books and manuscripts stored neatly on old shelves. The second is a piled-up mess of parchment. "My grandfather, who was an intellectual, read these works," Maygala told the French newspaper Le Monde. "My father wasn't interested so he just locked them up here."

The Kounati Badindi collection boasts treatises on astrology and astronomy, illustrated zodiacs and sky maps offering priceless insights into Islamic cosmology. Maygala was keen to stress that books in private hands have served a useful educational purpose right up until the present day. "These libraries have always been living," he told Le Monde. "You tell me that the manuscripts are worth hundreds and thousands of Euros, but the knowledge they hold is inestimable. I haven't really inherited anything. These books have simply been passed down to me by my father, so that one day I can pass them on to my eldest son."

The old patriarch of the Ben Essayouti clan, which has provided the Djinguereber mosque in Timbuktu with its imams since days of old, kept his family library under lock and key for years. Even his nephew, Abdramane Ben Essayouti, wasn't allowed to see them. "It took me years to persuade my uncle to liberate the manuscripts and offer their wisdom to humanity rather than to the termites," he told Le Monde. "I kept telling him that every time a manuscript was lost, it was a story that died." Months before his uncle passed away, Abdramane was finally given access to the dusty old vault. There he found 8,000 manuscripts heaped together in an unholy disorder.

There were not only Qurans that were half a millennium old but also translations of the Greek philosophers, books of alchemical spells and esoteric charms, and treatises on magic that combined Islamic, Egyptian, Moorish and Kabbalistic teachings. With the help of SAVAMA, imam Ben Essayouti has been devoting a large proportion of his waking hours to running the family library, conserving the manuscripts and unlocking the knowledge that like within them, like precious stones hidden deep in seams of recalcitrant rock.

Another important collection traces its origins back to the Visigoths, the Germanic hordes who swept into Spain as the Roman Empire crumbled in the 5th century and settled there.

After the Arabo-Berber invasion of the 8th century, those Spanish Visigoths became known as *Qutis* in Arabic. A certain Ali bin Ziyad bin al-Mutawakkil al-Quti was driven from his home in Toledo by the Castilian *reconquista* of al-Andalus after the great fire of 1467 and travelled across the great desert to the land of the blacks. In his luggage was a set of exquisite manuscripts, written in Arabic for the most part. Al-Quti married a noble woman of the ruling Askia dynasty of the Songhai, in other words a black African woman. Their son, Mahmoud al-Quti, was half African, half Islamicised European. He also married an Askia, this time the niece of the Emperor and, although they were at times marginalised because of their foreign Christian ancestry, the al-Qutis became renowned administrators and *qadis,* or judges, in Timbuktu and Gao.

Today the *Fondo Kati* and the *Biblioteca Kati*, comprising the al-Quti, or 'Ka'ti' family collection, is one of the greatest libraries in Timbuktu. It contains over 12,000 manuscripts, about half of which are held in the central Kati library and half dispersed amongst the various branches of the family. Professor John Hunwick has likened the Kati collection to the Dead Sea Scrolls in terms of their importance. The earliest work in the collection is a Quran written on vellum by a scribe in the town of Ceuta in 1198. Its latest works were copied for the Kati family in the 19th century. The Fondo's most famous possession is the *Tarik al-Fattash*, a chronicle of the Songhai Empire written either by Mahmoud al-Ka'ti or his grandson Ibn al-Mukhtar, no one is quite sure which, sometime in the late 1650s or 1660s. Along with the *Tarik as-Sudan*, the *Tarik al-Fattash* remains one of the greatest primary sources of West African history, as essential to the northern Malian sense of identity as the Venerable Bede's *Ecclesiastical History of the English People* is to the English.

The Fondo Kati's director, Ismaël Dadië Kati, explained to the Malian newspaper Lafia Révélateur that the major part of the Kati collection is made up of books belonging either to Ali bin Ziyad bin al-Muttawakil al-Ka'ti or the Emperor Askia Mohammed himself, both of whom were great collectors and patrons of learning. Other books were acquired or copied by later generations of the Kati family.

There are also manuscripts with no family connection, including a trove of documents written by or about the *morisco* or Jewish families from Andalusia who settled in Timbuktu after the reconquista. The Fondo Kati, which is financed by Spain, contains works in Arabic, Hebrew and *Aljamiado*, medieval Spanish written in Arabic script. "The last city of Andalus is neither Malaga nor Algeciras," Ismaël Dadië Kati told a journalist from Ahram Online, "it is Timbuktu."

All these books, manuscripts, letters and piles of paper are the legacy of one of the most intellectually fertile periods in African history. At the apogee of its power in the 16th century, the great scholarly houses and Quranic schools of Timbuktu were full of students, tens of thousands of them. They all needed books in order to learn. Without printing technology, the only way to feed that demand was to copy texts by hand, again and again and again. So Timbuktu developed a thriving scribing industry. 'Master' copies arrived in Timbuktu with the caravans from Damascus, Cairo, Fez, Meknes, Toledo and other distant places. From about the 14th century onwards, new books were also written in Timbuktu and nearby towns such as Djenne, Diakha and Kabara. Copies were then commissioned by wealthy families, imams, cadis, *madrassas* and village headmen. Books were also bought and sold on the open market. They were objects of great prestige whose market value exceeded in relative terms that of gold, salt or slaves, the other mainstays of the Timbuktu economy.

As objects, the manuscripts are beautiful and rare but the knowledge within them is rarer still. Its breadth defies expectation. If all of Timbuktu's books were to be collected in one place and one was allowed to roam freely in amongst them, or sit down and consult the catalogues of this fantasy library, the range of subjects on display would be astounding.

First there are the copies of the Quran, gathered from different centuries and different parts of the Muslim world. Then you move on to the lives of the Prophet, the books of the hadith, the commentaries on the Quran and the hadith, the books of *fiqh* or jurisprudence covering all the main *madh'hab* or legal schools, the legal commentaries and the critiques of different judgements and legal interpretations.

Then, leaving aside purely religious and legal texts for a moment, there are thousands of treatises that examine all branches of what might now be called the humanities; history, geography, poetry, languages, grammar, music, architecture and philosophy, both Arabic and Greek in translation. There are books about general science, medicine, pharmacology, anatomy, botany, zoology, astronomy, chemistry, mathematics and geometry.

Then come the books on pseudo-scientific and spiritual subjects such as astrology, alchemy, spells, numerology, charms, Kabbalistic teaching and magical formulas. There are tomes that give advice on how to run society, covering subjects such as agriculture, livestock management, politics, good governance, tolerance, the rights of man, the rights of women, the rights of children and inter-communal affairs.

And last, there are all the administrative and personal archives containing letters, diaries, accounts, bills of transaction, wills, mortgages, deeds to water supplies and palm groves and miscellaneous family papers. All of this material is written not only in Arabic, Hebrew and *Aljamiado*, but also in local languages such as Tamashek, Fulani and Songhoi rendered in Arabic script.

As a final bonus, there are the 'notes'; the endless marginal scribblings that sometimes feature erudite analysis of the main texts, or even partial or complete transcriptions of other texts – two books in one as it were – and sometimes more mundane comings and goings. A unique feature of the Timbuktu manuscripts is that this enormous wealth of written material was created by a society that had no printing presses and didn't manufacture its own paper, which was generally imported from southern Europe. It was a precious commodity in late medieval Timbuktu. There was always vellum of course, but curing and treating animal skins was a time-consuming and expensive business. Wood bark was plentiful but offered a poor and fragile writing surface. So when paper was lacking, scribes and book owners simply wrote in the margins of existing books, turning many of these ancient volumes into a kind of evolving receptacles of knowledge. The ephemera of late medieval and early modern Sahelian society is squeezed into those margins, warts and all. It is a historical resource without pair in Africa.

Therein lay the fear, not in the books themselves but their subject matter. Bibliophiles can be thankful that The Prophet never issued any edicts against books per se, or that none of his actions even gave a hint that books were *haram*, a hint that might then have become part of the hadith and consequently mainstream Islamic law. But the danger was that Timbuktu's Islamist occupiers might end up objecting to the very openness and broad enlightenment of the subjects contained in the Timbuktu manuscripts. There was also a fear that they might destroy the manuscripts just to hit the West's most sensitive spot with a hammer and snub its petty cultural anxieties.

In May 2012, the old offices of The Ahmed Baba Institute in Timbuktu were pillaged by mujahedeen of AQIM and Ansar ud-Dine. Computers, scanners and other conservation equipment were taken. 4x4 vehicles belonging to the institute were also stolen from outside the brand new Institute building, upon which Khadafy and Thabo Mbeki had lavished so much coin. Nonetheless, thankfully, neither the offices inside, nor the vaults holding up to 20,000 books were touched. Most of the Institutes' staff and guardians had fled Timbuktu in April and the lack of surveillance left the manuscripts in the library dangerously exposed. The same was true for other smaller libraries, including the Mamma Haidara Memorial Library, the Ben Essayouti Library and the Fondo Kati.

Nonetheless, as soon as it became clear that Timbuktu would fall into the hands of the various rebel groups, the custodians of the Timbuktu manuscripts began to transfer their treasures out of the main library buildings and into more secret and remote locations, just as they had done during countless moments of tension and war in preceding decades and centuries. The Fondo Kati reported that 8,000 of its manuscripts had been hidden away for safekeeping. Collections were dispersed and scattered once again. It was hoped that the job of reuniting them when peace returned would not be as arduous as it has been in the past. Some also clung to the hope the manuscripts would be protected by the Touareg reverence for books, which are considered rare treasures in their nomadic culture.

As long as AQIM controlled Timbuktu and the surrounding region, however, the danger remained. After all, Libyan Salafists had already torched a library full of ancient manuscripts in the town of Zlitan earlier in 2012. Refugees from Timbuktu who were interviewed by Amnesty International in Bamako reported that an Ansar ud-Dine spokesman had declared certain topics in the city's ancient manuscripts to be impious.

"The people from Ansar ud-Dine told us that some of the books in the Ahmed Baba Institute didn't conform with Islam and that we should refer to books that they themselves had bought with them," they said. The bearded ones probably hadn't been referring to the 16th century recipe for toothpaste nor the 19th century advice on how to treat snakebite with toad meat or soothe boils with panther droppings. Nor to the endless analyses and dissections of Islamic law which, after all, form the bulk of the subject matter in the manuscripts. But they might well have been referring to the advice given to women on how to deal with menstruation, or to books of sensuous love poetry or to the volumes discussing the rights of man, the responsibilities of rulers, the need for tolerance and related enlightened philosophies.

Saadou, an archivist at the Ahmed Baba Institute who fled from Timbuktu to Bamako on a pirogue down the Niger River, a gruelling five-day journey in the high heat of summer, told La Vie Magazine that "normally the state looks after those kinds of cultural riches. But since the arrival of the rebels, the state no longer exists in Timbuktu. If the men who were protecting the manuscripts and who know their value are in danger, then the manuscripts themselves are in danger. For the rebels, they're nothing but insignificant bits of paper…"

"I have no faith in the rebels," declared Professor Shamil Jeppie from the University of Cape Town, one of the directors of the Timbuktu Manuscript Project. "They have an educated leadership, but they are sending in foot soldiers who are illiterate and if they want something they will take it. They won't have any respect for paper culture."

The assumption that the intellectual wonders contained in the manuscripts of Timbuktu meant nothing to the foot soldiers of Al Qaida had a certain snobbish ring to it, but it was undoubtedly true in part. Many of the Islamist grunts in northern Mali were illiterate nomads from the northern deserts who had enlisted mainly in order to feel secure and purposeful in the bosom of a large and well-funded guerrilla army.

Culture was not their primary concern. In fact, for the most part, it didn't even figure on their list of concerns at all. Other members of AQMI and MUJAO however, especially some of the foreign fighters from Mauritania, Tunisia, Libya, Algeria and elsewhere, were well educated. Some even had university degrees and diplomas. They were no doubt well aware of the cultural value of the ancient manuscripts, but their hard line Salafi beliefs also balked at the enlightenment and broad spirit of enquiry the books embodied.

Therein lay a stark contradiction. The common plaint of AQIM emirs is that a satanic coalition of Jews, Crusaders, corrupt Arab leaders and infidels has purposefully robbed Islam and Islamic culture of the glory it once knew in bygone centuries. They often quote the Andalusia of the Middle Ages as a prime example of this cultural rape, and yet they revile the very tolerance and open-mindedness that made Andalusia great. The manuscripts of Timbuktu presented an intriguing dilemma to the more culturally aware Islamist leaders in the city. Should they be preserved as a literary monument to the greatness of Islam in Africa? Or should they be destroyed as the purveyors of sinful ideas?

Another anxious possibility was that the Islamists would perceive an altogether different kind of value in the manuscripts. A busy black market trade in ancient Islamic texts is thriving in Europe, the Middle East, North America and elsewhere. Some of the rarer books in the Timbuktu libraries would fetch considerable sums on this market and even more if they were split up and flogged off as single pages. "It is very possible that in a few weeks, we'll find the Timbuktu manuscripts on sale throughout the world," said Marc Geoffrey, a researcher at the Institute for the Research and History of Texts, in an interview he gave to La Vie in the summer of 2012. "Most of them haven't been catalogued which means that we don't know what's in them, how old they are and what they contain. Whereas, each manuscript is a unique object which potentially contains very rare work. It is a whole swathe of African and Arabo-Muslim history that could disappear…"

There was also a concern that if the international community made too great a fuss over the manuscripts, the jihadists would destroy them just to punish the West for its arrogance, its meddling in the affairs of Islam and its all too precious anxiety for inanimate objects of merely cultural importance. This, after all, was certainly part of the motivation behind the tomb-storm in Timbuktu at the beginning of July 2012. "One must be very careful not to provoke them," was the advice of Abdel Kader Haidara, who claimed to have received assurances from AQIM's spokespeople that the manuscripts wouldn't be harmed. Under Abdel Kader Haidara's aegis, the Libraries of Timbuktu issued a combined declaration on 18th June 2012 confirming that none of the manuscripts had been threatened, nor any person looking after them harmed. However, the declaration did concede that the presence of armed groups in the city put the manuscripts in danger.

For ten tense months, the community of owners, funders, historians, librarians, researchers and archivists to whom the manuscripts of Timbuktu represented a peerless treasure and the fruit of decades of painstaking labour, watched the unfolding tragedy in northern Mali with mounting anxiety. The leaders of AQIM and Ansar ud-Dine held part of Africa's memory in their hands. Did they know it? Did they resent the value that the world saw in it? Did they care?

On the morning of January 28th 2013, they thought they had the answer. News broke that AQIM mujahedeen had set fire to the new Ahmed Baba institute building and another library, as a parting gift to the advancing 'crusaders'. According to Timbuktu's mayor Hallé Ousmane Cissé, a "devastating blow." "This is terrible news," he told The Guardian newspaper. "The manuscripts were a part not only of Mali's heritage but the world's heritage. By destroying them they threaten the world. We have to kill all of the rebels in the north."

Predictably, the international reaction was one of shock and outrage. "I'm absolutely devastated, as everybody else should be," Essof Pahad, the South African chairman of the Timbuktu manuscript project, told The Guardian. "I can't imagine how anybody, whatever their political or ideological leanings, could destroy some of the most precious heritage of our continent. They could not be in their right minds. The manuscripts gave you such a fantastic feeling of the history of this continent. They made you proud to be African. Especially in a context where you're told that Africa has no history because of colonialism and all that. Some are in private hands but the fact is these have been destroyed and it is an absolute tragedy."

As the hours and days passed, however, the story became more nuanced. Footage of the burned out Ahmed Baba library, with its sorry heaps of discarded manuscript cases, flashed across TV and computer screens across the world. But it seemed that the old strategy of dispersal had worked its magic and saved the manuscripts, or most of them at least. They were safely stored in underground caches, remote caves or the cupboards and backrooms of private houses. Some had even been secreted away to safety in Mopti and other southern towns. Abdel Kader Haidara, who had fled to Bamako just weeks before the liberation of Timbuktu, told Canada's Globe & Post newspaper that the manuscripts were indeed safe.

The word 'preservation' means different things at different times. For years the work of preservation had been going on in the air conditioned offices of the Ahmed Baba Institute and in other libraries, where men and women wearing white gloves had patiently scanned book after book, coating their pages in protective cellophane, removing termites and bugs and then housing them in boxes specially made by local craftsmen.

Throughout 2012, preservation meant secretly transferring thousands of books into sacks, crates, boxes and metal trunks, loading them up in 4x4s, braving gun-toting mujahedeen patrols and checkpoints and then stashing them away in secret locations throughout a 500 mile radius. It was preservation work that demanded extreme courage, sang-froid and dedication to the immense material and symbolic value of those old books.

Abdel Kader Haidara organised a team of people to save the works in the Mamma Haidara Memorial library. Imam Ben Essayouti did the same for his family collection and many others risked their lives in this feat of collective heroism. Africa's memory has been preserved, at least until the next wave of invaders hits Timbuktu.

17. "Flames over the heart of the damned"

Writers, poets and the media in modern day Mali

"Just as in Afghanistan, their [the Islamists'] aim is to completely efface all traces of civilisation and therewith the memory of their victims, that's to say Mali, even Africa as a whole," wrote the Malian author Ousmane Diarra in an article entitled *Tombouctou le Martyre* ('Timbuktu the Martyr') that appeared on the Terangaweb website in April 2012.

"Even worse, part of their devilish intention is to destroy everything which, in cultural terms, links black Africa to white Africa. In that regard, they constitute a threat not only to Mali but to African unity full stop. In black Islam the cult of the saints, a practice that came originally from Islam in the Maghreb, is a key element. It is a tolerant open Islam, a harmonious syncretism between monotheism and the veneration of ancestors inherited from the traditional negro-African religions. The acts of these new barbarians… affect me not only inasmuch as they're an attempt to destroy my country, my civilisation, but also as a profanation of my most intimate being, my deepest soul, a destruction of my memory, my intelligence and all that my ancestors invented in order that I could be deemed a part of humanity because, thanks to my own creative spirit, I have invented something for humanity."

Diarra continues in an ominous, self-exonerating tone: "I saw this catastrophe coming. I described it in my books. I denounced it in my talks. Now it has come to pass. They want to empty me of my soul and 'a man without a soul is a like an empty envelope that anybody can fill with anything they like'," he writes, quoting a line from his own novel *Pagne de Femme* (ed. Gallimard 2007).

On April 23rd 2012, just weeks into the Islamist occupation of the north, the literary community of Bamako came together to celebrate the 17th *Journée internationale du livre et du droit d'auteur*, the International Book and Copyright Day. The event was organised by Malivaleurs and the Malian branch of PEN International, the global body that promotes the freedom of literary expression.

The tragedy of the north loomed heavily over the gathering. Expressions of outrage and grief over the new barbarianism flying the flag of Salafist Islam over Timbuktu, Gao and Kidal were heated and insistent. What proved more awkward, even painful, was an awareness that Malian writers, like some of their musical counterparts, had not been courageous and robust enough in their defence of democracy, good governance and the essential values of Malian culture in recent years. Malian writers and intellectuals had, with notable exceptions, sleep walked into disaster along with the mass of the Malian population. Too many had allowed themselves to compromise with *le système* or had been constrained to do so.

The *Journée du Livre* involved a large number of writers, intellectuals and institutional cultural organisations and offered panels on the themes of literature in education, defending the Timbuktu manuscripts and the threat to cultural heritage. Presiding over the meeting was the Malian filmmaker and ex minister of culture Cheick Oumar Sissoko.

"Writers of Mali! Have you documented Mali enough to put our country beyond the reach of danger from what is happening today?" he demanded to know from the assembled writers. Ismalia Samba Traoré, President of PEN-Mali and founder / director of the Malian publisher *Éditions La Sahélienne* made a passionate plea to Mali's literary world to engage in the crisis and help heal the country's wounds.

"We writers are amongst those who will rebuild Mali," he is reported to have said by the Malian newspaper Le Républicain, "and we will take an active part in the polemic that contradicts the numerous lobbies, university professors and media that feed on our divisions. We must be first in line to commit the facts and events that our country is living through to paper and make sure that Malian writers and analysts are best placed to enlighten national and international opinion [on these events]."

Ismalia Traore then went on to say that all Malians had to ask themselves a number of soul-searching questions: How can communities that have been torn apart be coaxed back into a dialogue about peace, civility and communal life? How can the concepts of respect and tolerance, of the inviolability of people and goods be translated into citizen action? How can Malians relate to each other despite social and political divisions, in strict respect of human rights? How to rebuild the country once peace returns, on principles of good governance that are accepted by all?

Mali has often been praised for its relatively free and vociferous press and media. Its media landscape blossomed after the overthrow of the military dictator Moussa Traore and the advent of multi-party democracy in 1992. The venerable government-backed daily *L'Essor*, founded at independence by the ruling RDA party and used by Traore as the official mouthpiece of his one-party state, was joined by a number of other private French language papers and magazines including *L'Aurore, Le Républicain, Info Matin, Les Echos, L'Independent, Nouvel Horizon* and *Soir de Bamako*. Even in the dark days of the military dictatorship, certain journalists were fondly appreciated for their daring metaphorical satire, especially in the pages of the state-run magazine *Sunjata.*

The profusion of new privately owned dailies and weeklies that appeared in the late 1980s and early 1990s provoked debate among the minority literate classes. Meanwhile the liberation of the airwaves bought a new wave of independent commercial, community and rural radio stations into being, broadcasting in all the diverse local languages of the Republic and thereby involving the less literate masses in the media debate. The same plurality has been lacking in the Malian tv landscape where the state-owned broadcaster *ORTM* holds on to both its monopoly and its insistence on broadcasting for the most part in Bamanan and French whilst paying mere lip service to minority languages such as Fulani, Dogon, Hassaniya and Tamashek. Malians with the necessary means tend to circumvent ORTM by tuning into the French channel *TV5* Monde and the multinational African channel *Africable.* However, it must also be said that ORTM was relieved of direct state control after the liberalisation of Mali's airwaves in 1992 and did much to help set up and promote the rural and community radio movement.

At the beginning of the new millennium the Internet began to take off, especially after the private Telecoms company Ikatel was taken over by the multinational Orange and broadband access increased exponentially whilst plummeting in price. Malian news websites such as the ORTM-run *Maliactu*, the news aggregator *Malijet* and the news sites *Malikounda* and *Journal du Mali* offered the world unprecedented access to Malian news and affairs. *Kidal.info* did the same for the Touareg dominated north east of the country.

Like the rest of Africa, Mali has discovered social networking and Facebook in a major way. During the current crisis, Facebook has been glowing red hot with debates and discussions fuelled by participants from all sections of Malian society, in all its local languages, with all its multi-ethnic wisdom and ancient prejudices posted in stark relief for the whole world to see.

Malians love to talk and debate. A pre-colonial esteem for learning and literacy has been boosted by the elevated respect for the intellectual so characteristic of French culture. From the informal *grins* of its city streets, where peer groups gather to chat, drink tea, and pass the time of day, through the endless arguments and counter-arguments on Facebook and other social networking sites, to the long exhaustive articles and tracts of writers, professors, analysts and commentators, Mali shows no lack of intellectual muscle and energy.

The proud hope of the Malian intellectual is that this appetite for debate and free discourse is now so securely rooted in Malian culture that it cannot easily be removed or suppressed by military dictators, power-hungry politicians, sanctimonious imams or Islamist emirs.

"The problem for them [the Islamists]," claims the rapper Amkoullel, "is that it is going to be very difficult because we live in a world in which new technologies have developed. They're in a country in which there are artists who are committed to protest, who speak up, there are rappers and also others. There are many ways in which to fight against those people."

Nonetheless, according to Cheick Oumar Sissoko and others, the vaunted freedom of the Malian press has at times been just as illusory as the good health of Malian democracy. "Even journalists have often been on the side of power," he tells me. "That's who pays them. They haven't been courageous enough. Writers have also admitted that they weren't watchful enough to really analyse the situation that was brewing in recent years. They recognised this during the meetings we held to discuss our heritage and now they're writing a lot."

In truth, a casual perusal of Mali's daily press output offers the extremes of both very good and very bad journalism. At the more positive end of the scale there are journalists such as Adam Thiam of *Le Républicain*, Mahamadou Camara of *Journal du Mali* or Ahmed Baba of RFI. Thiam's analyses of his country's misfortunes are especially good and often hilariously funny. But at the other end of the scale the unquestioning vitriol and lazy received wisdom is reminiscent of Europe's gutter press, especially the British 'red tops'.

Northern Mali is a hard territory for any outsider to understand properly and that goes for southern Malians too. There's some black, and some white, but also an awful lot of grey, and the endless reporting in both the national and international media that ignores that grey, treating it as a mere inconvenience, is dispiriting.

As for radio, Mali can be thankful that nothing as vicious as Rwanda's *Radio Libre des Mille Collines* has reared its ugly head during the recent crisis. Nonetheless, destructive demagoguery hasn't been entirely absent from Malian airwaves. The controversial Presidential candidate Oumar Mariko and his SADI party, who many accuse of provoking the brutal assault on the Koulouba Palace and the subsequent hospitalisation of President Dioncounda back in May 2012, has been using his privately owned *Radio Kayira* to fuel tension and social animosity among southern Malians.

As I write, unconfirmed reports are coming in that radio stations in Timbuktu and other northern cities have been calling for a witch-hunt against Arab and Touareg Islamist collaborators, calls which inevitably result in the loss of innocent lives.

There have also been many instances of responsible, even heroic, radio coverage. Not least among these is the case of Abdoul Malick Aliou Maiga, a journalist working for *Radio Adar Khoïma* in Gao. On August 4th 2012, the MUJAO took control of Aadar Khoïma's airwaves to announce that henceforth they intended to implement the ultimate sanction proscribed by Shari'a law in cases of theft. The first amputation would take place the next day on the Place de l'Indépendence, they said. The announcement provoked a demonstration the next morning by a crowd of locals who occupied the Place de l'Indépendence in attempt to prevent the amputation from happening. Aliou Maiga and his team from Aadar Khoïma were out on the streets covering events.

That evening he returned to the radio station to deliver a report on the situation for the 8 o'clock news. Just as he was about to go on air, a group of MUJAO enforcers turned up at Aadar Khoïma's studio and proceeded to abuse Aliou Maiga verbally and physically, accusing him of "mobilising the youth to prevent the application of shari'a law." They gun-butted him several times and then left him unconscious two hours later in front of Gao's main hospital. The doctor reported that his body was covered with bruises and wounds, some of which were to the head. He had been lucky to survive.

Meanwhile in the south, many Malian journalists and commentators have been all too willing to accept government and army sources as gospel since the beginning of the crisis and allow their humiliation and anger to explode in vitriolic print. Few have taken the necessary cold shower and analysed the sickness in the Malian body politic that lead to the crisis with honesty and courage.

Theories, some worthy of further investigation, others belonging to the realm of fantasy, swirled around like grit in a dust storm; Mali's demise is a Western plot to break up the country into malleable chunks, re-colonise it and seize the natural resources that lie as yet unexploited beneath its vast northern steppes. Or perhaps it is just a French plot, or a French and Qatari plot, or a French and American plot, or an Algerian plot, or a Burkinabé plot, or a plot brewed up by the ECOWAS nations, or the African Union or all of these in devilish union. Mali is hurt, bewildered, lost and rudderless and unsurprisingly perhaps, the press has mirrored those feelings perfectly at times.

Hidden away in that sandstorm of emotions, there has also been a genuine desire to analyse and understand the root causes of the crisis. The more honest and perceptive journalists and intellectuals have delved deep into the source of the country's pain. Yes, the great powers of the world have strategic interests in the Sahel. Yes, the Touareg, or a significant Touareg fringe, exploited the opportunities offered by the demise of the Ghadafy regime to act out the latest painful episode in a fifty year long struggle for self-determination. Yes, a violent militant jihadi movement, born in Algeria in the 1990s, which had taken root in the north of the country for a variety of uncomfortable reasons, also took advantage of the Libyan arms bonanza. But those bitter developments were only the pus-filled boils on the body of a much vaunted African democracy that had been failing its people for years, brought low by corruption, nepotism, self-interest, incompetence and weakness.

Once the country's worst nightmare became cold fact, the questioning, the urgency and the desperate need for answers re-energised some Malian writers and intellectuals, rappers and musicians. Their quest wasn't only to understand what had happened and why it happened, but to try and define the values that were worth the sacrifice of Malian blood.

If the Malian media in general lacked courage in the past, the crisis offered an opportunity to find it again. In early May 2012, Birama Fall, the director of the magazine *Le Prétoire*, was arrested in his office by a group of armed men and interrogated at the State Security building for four hours. On May 24th it was the turn of the publisher of the daily paper *22 Septembre*, Chahana Takiou, to be hauled up in front of the *Securité Militaire*. In June, armed men invaded the Bamako offices of the satellite channel Africable to halt the broadcast of an interview with a leader of the MNLA.

At around the same time, Abdrahamane Keita, the Editor-in-Chief of the daily paper *L'Aurore* was accosted and roughed up by armed men whilst walking in the street. They stole his mobile phone and one million CFA that he happened to be carrying on his person, leaving him battered and bruised on the sidewalk. In an article on this arbitrary curtailment of press freedom, the newspaper 22 Septembre commented that "the freedom of the press in Mali, dearly earned through struggle, at the price of blood and tears in March 1991 and set in stone in our Constitution of February 25th 1992, is now more than ever threatened by a shadowy armed force that is using the methods of a state militia belonging to another regime and another era."

On July 12th, following the publication of several editorials criticising Captain Sanogo and his putchistas, Saouti Haidara, publisher of the daily *L'Indépendent*, was arrested by ten armed men, bundled into a 4x4 vehicle and taken away for interrogation. He was found several hours later near Bamako's 26 Mars Stadium with bruises all over his head and arms. One of the arresting soldiers was overheard telling Mr Haidara that "you journalists are a pain in our arses!" The Malian Union of Press and Communication Workers issued a staunch condemnation of the acts of aggression and intimidation perpetrated against journalists and newspaper editors by supporters of Captain Sanogo's military junta.

Some Malian writers also rediscovered a courageous sense of purpose. When I interviewed Cheick Omar Sissoko in October 2012, he was keen to stress that there was an urgent desire amongst Mali's intellectual class to document and dissect the crisis. He cited authors like Professor Issa N'Diaye of Bamako University, whose writing pulled no punches and who, in fairness, had never been afraid to speak out in the past.

One of his articles, entitled *Mali – A 'democracy' against the people*, published at the end of May 2012, opened with the line "The brutal fall of ATT [ex-President Amadou Toumani Toure] has left the rotten foundations of a Malian democracy so lauded by outsiders completely naked."

N'Diaye went on to criticise the 'game' of democratic legitimacy which the Western powers are so happy to play in Africa, giving elections their stamp of approval when they are riddled with irregularities. "Meanwhile," he wrote, "Malian men and women have never despised their leaders and the political classes so much."

Cheick Oumar Sissoko also mentioned the writer Doumbi Fakoly, a tireless promoter of Panafricanism, African pride and a neo-pagan religion called Kemetism, which is based on traditional African animism and ancient Egyptian beliefs. Fakoly has written over thirty books, including several that denounce the racism inherent in The Bible and The Quran. He has also criticised the misuse and misrouting of power after the overthrow of Mali's military dictatorship in March 1991.

In July 2012, Fakoly wrote an open letter to interim Prime Minister Cheick Modibo Diarra which opened with the line "This open letter is the echo of the voiceless who despair to see you at work; the salutary work of restoring our dignity, which has been seriously damaged by your timid management of the painful events that have beset our country."

Days after the first desecration of the Sidi Mahmoud mausoleum in Timbuktu, on May 4th, Malivaleurs called a meeting at the La Medina cultural centre in Bamako to launch their campaign to save the manuscripts of Timbuktu in particular and the cultural heritage of the north in general. It was attended by many of the intellectual luminaries of Mali; writers, journalists, historians, cultural activists, library owners and archivists. A sumptuously produced documentary by the South African film-maker Zola Maseko entitled *The Manuscripts of Timbuktu* was projected and the declaration that opens Part 2 of this book was read out and endorsed.

The indefatigable Ismaila Samba Traore, head of the Malian publishing house *Éditions La Sahélienne* and founder of Malivaleurs, issued a challenge whose emotional force was undiminished by the irony of his own powerlessness in the matter: "From this time onwards," he said, "we hold the armed groups accountable for all the crimes and violations of rights. We hold them responsible for all acts against our heritage. From this day forth we constitute the civilian opposition to the armed movements, their leaders and identifiable members."

Ismaila Samba Traore founded *Malivaleurs* in April 2012 to define and promote the cultural values of Mali and realign the country's political and social life with those values. Respect is at the heart of the Malivaleurs philosophy; respect for difference, for one's neighbour, for ethnic diversity, for family and human relations, democracy, national institutions and the physical and cultural wealth that the nation holds in common. Like most ordinary Malian citizens, Malivaleurs would like to see corruption eradicated and peace triumph and it has been organising conferences and debates in Mali to promote those aims. It also hopes to do the same in neighbouring countries like Niger, Burkina Faso and Mauritania.

In line with Traore's conviction that Malians themselves should take a lead in documenting the current crisis and explaining it to the world, La Sahélienne launched a new series of publications in November 2012 called *Regards sur une crise* (Views Of A Crisis). "It isn't right that other people, especially heads of state, should talk and decide in the name of the Malian people," Ismaila Samba Traore told the newspaper *L'Indicateur du Renouveau.* "Everything is being discussed and decided on our behalf. We writers had to react to this state of affairs."

The series includes works such as *Le Patriote et le Jihadiste* ('The Patriot and the Jihadi') by Mohammed Ag Erless and Djibril Koné; *L'Occupation du Nord* ('The Occupation of the North') by Doumbi Fakoly, Hamidou Magassa, Ciré Bâ and Boubacar Diagana; *Les Indignés de Kati* ('The Outraged of Kati') by Facoh Donki Diarra and *Réplique* ('Reply') by Salem Oulad El Hadje, Chirfi Moulaye Haidara, Mahmoud Zouber and Zeidane Ag Sidalamine. According to Traore, *Regards sur une crise* heralds the end of intellectual cowardice and resignation in Mali.

The writer Ousmane Diarra has never counted himself amongst the cowardly. "My entire intellectual struggle, right up until now, has consisted of warning people about this Islam that threatened us," he wrote to me in an email at the end of 2012, "and that threat was blindingly obvious. But smugly, not to say stupidly, everyone thought I was being too alarmist and nostalgic for my 'animism gone for ever.' No. I was secular of course, but I felt Islamic fanaticism coming towards us with the intention of settling here. I felt it in the sermons on the radio and on TV. After each of the five daily prayers, I heard words insulting non-Muslims, which they call *caffres.* I said that this wasn't right because verbal and moral violence always precedes physical violence. But nobody paid any attention. Even those people, intellectuals and others, who are all excited now, went along with it. The same people will be ready to collaborate with MUJAO and Ansar ud-Dine the day they arrive in Bamako. There was a blatant lack of courage, perhaps in an unconscious way. Even among certain rappers, who criticised politics without criticising society and the hypocrisy of the *ulemas.* It was easier then, and it is still easier now to criticise the President of the Republic that to criticise them [religious leaders]."

The point is well made. Scan the daily papers in Bamako and there's been no lack of criticism of interim President Dioncounda Traore, or the ex interim Prime Minister Cheikh Modibo Diarra, who was ousted by the military junta in December 2012 and replaced by the seasoned administrator Django Sissoko. Criticism of the military coup leader Captain Amadou Sanogo has also been in evidence. Rare are the voices however that have been raised against the High Islamic Council and its charismatic leader Mahmoud Dicko, or Ansar ud-Dine 'south', the vastly popular Islamic association founded by imam Cheikh Chérif Ousmane Madani Haidara (aka Wulibali or 'He who speaks the truth') 20 years before Iyad Ag Ghali and the AQIM rulers of Timbuktu co-opted the name. The same can be said the great imams of Nioro, such as the leader of Malian Tijaniya Sufis, Amadou Hady Tall, and the leader of the Hamalliya Sufis, Mohammed Ould Cheikha.

In a country in which traditional democratic politics are widely considered to have betrayed the people's trust and hopes, these religious leaders not only enjoy immense popular esteem, they also wield considerable political power. Heaping invective on the heads of Mali's beleaguered politicians has become a popular mass-participation sport. Taking apart Sanogo and his junta is more of a minority activity that requires a certain amount of courage and effrontery. Criticising the country's religious leaders however remains a risky pastime. They are among the few remaining public figures that still inject hope, respect and trust into the hearts of many millions of Malians.

The written word continues to wield its power in Mali, just as it did in the 'port' cities of the Sahel centuries ago. It reveals a country whose pride has been battered and whose compass has temporarily been lost. It reveals prejudice, paranoia, cowardice and stupidity, but also courage, honesty, insight and a desire to understand what has gone wrong. It reveals an attempt to define social values that have been temporarily obscured and must be revealed and cherished once again if Mali is to heal and prosper.

Last year, Editions La Sahélienne published two books of poetry by two young Malian poets: *Sanglots de la Joie* (Sobs of Joy) by Mohammed Hamady Coulibaly and *Les Larmes de la Tombe* (The Tears of the Tomb) by Aisha Diarra. Diarra's youth, beauty and air of keenly focussed conviction all paint a hopeful picture of Mali's future. That future resides in part in these young poets, in the rappers of Les Sofas de la République and Ça Suffit, in an educated middle class youth mercifully still devoid of cynicism, hungry to understand, primed with the desire to speak up, despite the silencing respect for elders that is both Mali's blessing and its curse.

"The rightful aim of literature is to help people to speak out on behalf of the poor and that's what we should be doing," Aisha Diarra said in an interview she gave to the state broadcaster ORTM: "Writing for the people, writing to liberate society."

The following are three poems taken from *Les Larmes de la Tombe* by Aisha Diarra, and reprinted here with my translations by kind permission of Éditions la Sahélienne and Aisha Diarra herself:

La lutte

Tant de jours ont chuté,
Mon âme trottine dans l'obscurité,
Pendant que les dirigeants entêtés
Dans leur soit disant bonté
Sèment partout la pauvreté,
Ces semences personne ne peut les compter,
Personne ne dit rien, malgré que tout le monde souffre
Dans la cité ;
Mais moi je vais parler
Car je suis un messager pour les effrontés.
C'est pour cela que je viens pour lutter
Comme une poule venue sauver
Son poussin, malgré sa petitesse est armée.
Oh ! Arbre qui m'a bercé,
Laissez-moi en ton ombre me reposer
Pour imiter l'oiseau qui a appris sans sa famille à chanter
Et regarder la nature qui caresse l'univers par sa beauté

(Taken from Les Larmes de la Tombe by Aicha Diarra, © Éditions La Sahélienne, 2012)

The Struggle

So many days have crumbled,
My soul trots along in obscurity,
While mule-headed leaders
In their so-called goodness
Scatter poverty all about them,
No one can count those seeds,
Nobody says anything. Everyone suffers
In the old town and housing estate ;
But I will speak out
For I'm a messenger for the brazen-hearted
That's why I've come to fight
Like a chicken who's come to save
Her chick, armed despite her tininess.
Oh Tree that cradled me!
Let me rest in your shade
To imitate the bird who learned to sing
Without the help of her family
And look at nature
Who, by her beauty, caresses the universe.
(Translated from the French by Andy Morgan)

Le droit

J’étais au sommet de la montagne
Me cachant de tout ce que je connais :
Homme, tristesse, solitude
Pour observer longuement
La misère qui est sur la terre
Et donner à mes pensées un peu d’eau.
Mon regard, sans ses tristes promenades,
Voit sur le sol des paysans fiers, ils cultivent le blé,
Mais en vérité, ils chassent la misère
Ils sont abandonnées, hélas !
Ils questionnent la révolution par un regard : « où est
Marx ? »
Ils se sentent seuls,
Ils demandent où est le seigneur.
Ils sont mi-athées,
C'est-à-dire sont presque comme Nietzsche qui demande
Après Dieu.
Non, je ne renoncerai pas à mes vers doux
Pour les proses de flamme comme Platon l’a fait.
Ni pour l’argent, ni pour tout l’or du monde
Car mes vers sont des flammes
Qui s’élèvent au dessus des cœurs des damnés
Car ils sont pierres que je lance aux injustes,
Ils sont pires que des aiguilles.
La douceur de mes vers est comme la sagesse de
Mohamed le messager
Mes vers sont des serpents
Qui sifflotent aux oreilles des pauvres :
« Battez vous pour votre droit, mourrez pour vos droits,
C’est la plus grande fierté »
Mes vers sont des vers de paix
Qui disent à Etéocle et Polynice : « unissez-vous. »

(Taken from Les Larmes de la Tombe by Aicha Diarra, © Éditions La Sahélienne, 2012)

Justice

I was on the mountaintop
Hiding from everything I know :
Man, sadness, solitude,
To observe for a long while
The misery that exists on earth
And give my thoughts a little water.
My gaze, without its melancholy strolling,
Looks out on the earth of proud peasants,
They're growing wheat,
But in truth, they're chasing misery
They are abandoned, alas!
They are questioning the revolution with a simple look:
"Where is Marx?"
They feel all alone,
They ask where the Lord might be.
They are half atheist.
That's to say, almost like Nietzsche, who asks
After God.
No, I will not renounce my gentle verses
For flaming prose, as Plato did.
Nor for money, nor all the gold in the world.
For my verses are flames in themselves
Which rise up over the hearts of the damned,
Or stones that I hurl at the unjust,
Worse than needles.
The gentleness and sweetness of my verses
Is like the wisdom

Of Mohammed the messenger.
My verses are like serpents
That hiss gently in the ears of the poor:
"Fight for your rights, die for your rights,
It is the greatest reason to be proud."
My verses are verses of peace
That say to Eteocles and Polynices: "Unite!"
(Translated from the French by Andy Morgan)

Les larmes des pauvres

Je suis loin des d'être un draconien,
Mais j'emmielle tout ce que je fais et ressens
Je ne l'ai pas encore dit,
Mais ce sont mes parents seuls
Qui sont mon grand amour.
Je pleure, mais oh ! Pauvres,
Ce sont tes larmes qui tombent de mes yeux.
Mon livre est un univers, ma poésie est une maison
Et mes strophes sont un grand matelas étalé.
Reposez vous dessus, s'il vous arrivait d'être esseulés.
Et nichez vous dans mon livre univers sans complexe.
Tous les jours sont maussades pour les pauvres.
Tous les dirigeants du Mali sont des narcisses.
Oh ! Toi qui médites sur mes véridiques strophes,
T'es-tu demandé de quoi se nourrissent les pauvres
Quand ils ont faim ? « De larmes » me dit un vieux
Fantôme.
Moi, je me suis posé cette question
Durant toute mon existence et je n'ai que 17 ans.
Certains ont 30 ans, 50 ans et d'autres 60, 70 ans
Et ne se sont jamais posé une seule fois
Cette question durant toute leur vie.
Mon dieu, ils ont vécu dans une existence nébuleuse.
Il y'a tant de choses que j'aimerais dire et faire.
Mais comment ?
De quoi se nourrissent mes strophes quand ils sont en
Colère ?
Elles se nourrissent d'amour, de vérité, d'angoisses et de
Larmes.
Et, moi, j'ai toujours emmiellé tout ce que j'ai et ressenti.

(Taken from Les Larmes de la Tombe by Aicha Diarra, © Éditions La Sahélienne, 2012)

The Tears of the Poor

I'm far from being draconian,
I honey all I do and feel,
I've never said it before
But my greatest love
Is for my parents and no other.
I cry, but oh! The poor,
Those are the tears that fall from my eyes.
My book is a universe, my poetry a house
And my strophes are a large mattress laid out.
Rest on it, if you happen to feel lonely.
And nestle down in my book, a universe with no complexes.
Every day is sullen for the poor.
All the leaders of Mali are narcissi.
Oh! You who meditate on my truthful strophes,
Have you every asked yourself on what the poor will feed
When they're hungry?
"On tears," says the old ghost.
As for me, I've asked myself this question
Throughout my existence, and I'm only seventeen.
Some are 30 years old, 50 and others 60 or 70
And they've never asked themselves this question
Not even once during their long lives.
Lord, they've lived a nebulous existence.
There are so many things I'd love to do and say,
But how?
On what do my strophes feed when they're angry?
They feed on love, on truth, on anguish and tears.
And as for me,
I've always honeyed all that I've done and felt.
(Translated from the French by Andy Morgan)

18. "A mirror of the people's aspirations"

Cinema and the political struggle in Mali

The script was simplicity itself; an old hermit who lives in a hut by the stately Niger River receives a few visitors and talks about his homeland. "Mali is a country blessed by God," the sage explains, "and that's why it has such a rich natural and cultural heritage. All its problems stem from egoism, meanness and the lack of solidarity shown by two types of people; the rich who refuse to share and those who hold on to power. All that's needed for the country to prosper is for these people to show some pity for their fellow countrymen."

When the 20-minute long documentary came to a close, the audience at the 9th edition of the *Rencontres Cinématographiques de Bamako* (RCB) which took place in the Malian capital on December 22nd 2012, erupted into wide-eyed applause. The moral depth and clairvoyance of the old man's words had soldered them to their seats. The raw truth behind the Malian tragedy of 2012 had just been sketched out for them with the simplest and clearest of strokes, right in front of their eyes, by an old and forgotten soothsayer a full 13 years before that tragedy happened. The one-day film festival had been blessed by many fine offerings from Mali and neighbouring countries but this simple documentary, entitled *The Sage of Ngolonina*, stole the show.

Before the documentary was screened Souleymane Cissé, Mali's greatest film director and the creator of *The Sage of Ngolonina*, took the stage to open the *Rencontres* and say a few words. He reminded his audience, which comprised filmmakers and film industry activists from West and North Africa as well as the Malian Minister of Culture and other eminent cultural figures, that the theme of the day was "The role of cinema in the culture of peace." The purpose was to ask pertinent questions about what film had done for the promotion of peace, and what it might do in the future. Not only film but culture in general. "Mali, confronted by the most serious crisis in its history, is in need of peace today," declared the seventy-year old director. "But meanwhile, every son and daughter of Mali must ask themselves if they have done, and done well, all they can for their country." Cissé added that, as a filmmaker, he wished to present his apologies to the nation for lacking the means to save it from catastrophe with his own moving images.

The day began with a series of short films by young Malian film-makers on various subjects relating to the crisis, all produced by the West African Union of Film and Audiovisual Creators and Entrepreneurs (UCECAO), a body that Cissé himself had set up in the mid 1990s in response to a growing crisis of funding and distribution that was crippling the West African film industry. Next up were documentaries by Ousmane Baye from Senegal and Tewfik Farès from Algeria, followed by a feature entitled *Korafola* by the Malian filmmaker Mamadou Cissé, which had recently won a jury mention at the Carthage Film Festival. The day closed with *Mama Africa*, Mika Kaurismaki's documentary about Miriam Makeba, and Cissé's own feature film *Waati*, which tells the story of Nandi, a black child living in apartheid South Africa who flees his homeland to live in Ivory Coast, Mali and Namibia. Interspersed amongst these films were forums and debates. The crisis energised the discourse. The emotional heat was high.

And, of course, there was that screening of *The Sage of Ngolonina.* The documentary coupled with the sombre mood of urgency provoked a great deal of soul-searching at the *Rencontres.* The general consensus was that the Malian film industry was undergoing its very own crisis. Few new films were being made and those that were, faced a brick wall when it came to distribution. Cinemas in Mali are almost non-existent. National TV pays almost nothing for screenings. All that's left is a few art house cinemas in Europe and America and the usual round of film festivals, which do wonders for kudos but precious little for the bottom line. The Malian director and President of the Union of Malian Film Directors Salif Traore, put it in the starkest of terms in his address to the meeting: "Malian cinema is going very badly."

In truth, the soul-searching had been going on for many years. A sclerotic sense of thwarted ambitions had descended on the Malian film industry in the mid-1990s. The vision of a vibrant and economically vital industry that could rival the printed press in its power to communicate ideas of social justice and fairness to all Malians, irrespective of their level of literacy, was getting hazier and weaker with every year that passed. The dream of a Malian Bollywood with a social conscience was evaporating along with sources of funding.

In an essay entitled *From the search for identity to political engagement*, the Malian film critic Moussa Bolly acknowledges that Malian films have improved in leaps and bounds in terms of technical quality, script and social engagement since the release of *Demain à Nanguila* by Joris Ivens and Moussa Sidibé, the first Malian film released after independence in 1960. Mali is the only African country to have produced three winners of the coveted *Étalon de Yennanga* (the equivalent of an African Oscar), at the annual Panafrican Film and Television Festival in Ouagadougou (FESPACO), the capital of Burkina Faso. The prize went to *Baara* (1979) and *Finyè* (1983) by Souleymane Cissé and *Guimba – Un Tyran, Une Époque* (1995) by Cheikh Oumar Sissoko.

A-list Malian directors and actors such as Souleymane Cissé, Cheikh Oumar Sissoko, Balla Moussa Keita, Falaba Issa Troare, Salif Traore and Adama Drabo have been screened and fêted at major film festivals around the world. Souleymane Cissé was 'discovered' by none other than

Martin Scorcese after he chanced on Cissé's masterpiece *Yeelen* (*Brightness*) as he was channel hopping in New York late one night. The movie entranced Scorcese and opened a new window on Africa Cinema for him. Scorcese met Cissé at a Film Festival in Paris and minted a solid professional relationship, inviting the Malian director to become a member of the Filmmaker's Council of his World Cinema Foundation. Nonetheless, peer-group recognition and seats of honour at film festivals, however assuaging for the creative ego though they may be, are no substitutes for a thriving and economically robust local film industry.

Malian cinema was born in the same atmosphere of social idealism, progress and rejection of colonial mentality as the country itself. The rights of workers, women, peasants, children and the poor were foremost in the minds of Malian cinema's pioneers. As Moussa Bolly puts it in his essay "It wasn't a matter of making 'cinema for cinema's sake', but of turning it into a tool with which to affirm independence and change. For them [Mali's formative film directors], cinema has to be an expression of the redoubtable power of language and the word, which has been so strongly anchored in Malian society since the time of the great empires."

In the early 1960s, Souleymane Cissé himself was simply a projectionist with vague ambitions to direct his own films when he happened to watch a documentary about the assassination of the Congolese leader Patrice Lumumba. "The arrest of Patrice Lumumba was determinant for my film career," he told the Algerian paper *L'Expression*. "It is that film that pushed me towards becoming involved in cinema." Cissé received a scholarship to study at the Institute of Higher Cinematographic Studies in Moscow. The newly independent Malian state maintained close contacts with Soviet Russia and the Eastern Bloc, contacts that were used to nurture and disseminate Malian cultural talent. Whilst Cissé was studying in Moscow, the great guitarist Ali Farka

Touré travelled to communist Bulgaria to perform his first ever concert outside Mali. Many Malian musicians, writers and artists studied in Cuba during the 1960s and 70s. Socialist convictions inspired the post-colonial African zeitgeist and Mali's creative industries were imbued with the overriding conviction that art had to serve the cause of social justice and progress or face the danger of becoming a bourgeois irrelevance. The film industry, inspired by Lenin's dictum that of all the arts, cinema is the most important, epitomised this belief.

With the overthrow of the socialist President Modibo Keita, and the arrival of the military dictator Moussa Traore in 1968, these ideals were slowly expunged from official discourse and policy. Nonetheless, they remained fixed in the hearts of Mali's filmmakers. Cissé's first full-length feature *Den Muso* (*The Young Girl*, 1975) told the story of a young mute girl who was raped by an unemployed man and then rejected by her family. It was banned by the Traore regime and Cissé was imprisoned on trumped up charges. His subsequent films, including *Finyé* (*The Wind*, 1982), about a student revolt against the military regime and his masterpiece *Yeelen*, all have some form of struggle for human rights and social justice at their core.

The same can be said for the movies of Adama Drabo, the former village schoolteacher and playwright who released his first film *Nieba, la journée d'une paysanne* (*Nieba, A Day in the Life of a Peasant*) in 1988 and followed it with the remarkable *Ta Dona!* (Fire!) in 1993. *Ta Dona!* is ostensibly a film about bush fires and environment damage. "But the film was also marked by the reawakening of economic and political life in a Mali that had been dominated by dictatorship for 23 years," Drabo told Moussa Bolly. "Those who read the scenario advised against any expression of this reality to avoid repression from the [military] regime. But it was a duty. As a director, I couldn't be indifferent to the search for peace by a people who were oppressed and humiliated every day."

Another of Drabo's films, *Taafé Fanga* (*Skirt Power*, 1997) is about a woman in a Dogon village who finds a mask that gives women power over men. The role and status of women in Malian society was a hot topic at the time. Many songs, released during the 1990s lauded the strength and resilience of Malian women, not least those sung by Oumou Sangaré, Mali's most famous female voice internationally and most vocal supporter of women's rights at home.

Cheick Oumar Sissoko's work is full of thinly veiled critiques of social and political injustice. *Guimba – Un tyran, un temps* (*Guimba – A Tyrant and his Time*, 1995) tells the story of Guimba, the tyrannical leader of a small Sahelian village in the Middle Ages and his loathsome dwarf son Janguine. The period atmosphere and narrative strength of the film draws inspiration from rural folk theatre and the long epic song cycles of Mali's griots or traditional bards. It plays out like a parable about totalitarianism and its transmission from one generation to the next, dressed up in the clothing of popular local culture and designed to be eminently digestible by the ordinary Malian.

Sissoko's other masterpiece is *Genèse* (*Genesis*, 1999), a film dedicated "To all those, throughout the world, who are victims of fratricidal conflict. To all those who are working for peace." In it, Sissoko transposes the Biblical struggle between Jacob the nomad, Hamor the farmer and Esau the hunter to Mali, a country where the tension between these three archetypes is still very much alive. If you strip the crisis of 2012 down to its essence you end up with a perennial, quasi archetypal, clash between the nomadic cultures of northern Mali, principally Arab and Touareg, and the sedentary agricultural cultures of the Niger River and lands further south, principally Songhai, Bambara, Malinké, Soninké and Khassonké. The hunters of Dogon and

Wassoulou complete the triptych, although their role is negligible in reality.

The Touareg 'problem' in Mali has its roots in the lack of affinity between the centralising socialist government that took control in 1960 and the free-ranging nomadic pastoralists with their decidedly un-socialist hierarchical clan structures, who lived in the north. The government in Bamako believed in a command and control agricultural policy, with five-year plans and fixed prices for produce and livestock. It was entirely geared towards boosting the productivity of sedentary agriculture and took little account of the small scale and, so the southerners believed, inefficient and backward methods of animal husbandry practiced by the Touareg and Arabs. Tension between these two ways of life led to open rebellion, repression and a cycle of violence that continues to this day. It is a conflict that is, in its essence, as old as that of Jacob, Hamor and Esau.

By the mid 1990s, however, it was clear that the early idealism and socialist fervour of the Malian film industry was flapping in the wind due to the crippling dearth of distribution, promotion and infrastructure. The country's few professional studios and editing suites were in a woeful state of disrepair. There were hardly any cinemas left and no distributors with the means and know-how to market a film properly. No money was forthcoming, either from international donors or from the Malian government, to help the industry back on its feet.

"Producing a film in Mali is a truly monumental task," Yusuf Coulibaly, the Director of the National Centre for Cinematographic Production, told Panapress in 2001. "A work rarely sees the light of day before four, five or even more years, thanks to a lack of finance, production infrastructure or distribution."

A lack of new films had already led to nose-diving cinema attendance figures, a trend that was accelerated by the increasing availability of pirated VHS copies and satellite TV. Furthermore, the government closed the National Cinematographic Office of Mali (OCINMA), an organisation that had hitherto managed to maintain a credible distribution and theatre network. Although the 20th edition of FESTPACO in 2007 was dedicated to Malian cinema, the fact that only one full-length Malian feature was screened at the festival, Salif Traore's *Faro, La Reine des Eaux*, was indicative of the underlying malaise.

So, in Mali's greatest hour of need, the country's film industry, like its army, has been in no fit state to respond effectively to the calamities facing the nation. Of course, making good films requires time and money and neither have been readily available. "Musicians have been vocal in their opposition to the problems that lead to this crisis, because they can write songs and respond rapidly and easily," Cheick Oumar Sissoko told me back in October 2012. "For cinema, it is more complicated. I know that right now La Direction Nationale du Cinéma is making two films about the crisis. Some young cameramen were sent north by Acte Sept to Timbuktu and Gao and they brought back images that we're in the process of editing. The director is a young guy called Aliou Konaté. But the difficulty is that we can't go up north with a proper team to film. All the places with sand are occupied now. And it is also a question of means. Mali was forced to leave the *OIF* (*Organisation Internationale de la Francophonie*). They're not financing our projects. I also fear that the EU won't be financing our projects. So it is very complicated."

The reality is simple: no money, no films. The military coup of March 22nd 2012 turned Mali into a pariah state, unworthy in the eyes of many international governments, donors and funders. Humanitarian, educational, scientific, economic projects of every stripe were left high and dry. Previous trickles of international money that kept a few Malian film projects alive became non-existent. The French intervention and the partial liberation of the north from Islamist occupation has brought International aid in its wake but with such a towering list of pressing priorities facing the country – holding elections, bringing back the refugees, making sure the harvests don't fail, restoring the shattered army and governmental institutions, rebuilding the pulverised infrastructure of northern cities etc etc – Malian cinema will have wait patiently at the back of the queue for the tiny sums that remain.

In the meantime, Malian film directors can do little else but attend festivals like FESTPACO, the Carthage Film Festival or the RCB and supplicate international funders whilst they mourn a vision that, although not entirely dead yet, is certainly struggling for survival. Like its music industry, Malian cinema was already in crisis before AQIM, Ansar ud-Dine and MUJAO raised their black banners over the north. Now it seems to be in intensive care. "No country can develop without crises," Souleymane Cissé told the audience at the RCB. "Crisis is part of our daily lives. But the way in which it is managed is crucial. It is important the Mali has a strong government and strong institutions." Perhaps he was too humble to add that a strong Malian film industry is also important, one that raises its head high and speaks to its own people in their time of direst need.

19. Showing another world

Kotéba and the 'Theatre of Resistance' in Mali

The popular philosophy of Malian people is often expressed in axioms and dictums. There are literally thousands of them. The *Acte Sept* Association was founded on just four:

- *A single finger cannot pick up a stone.*

- *If others wash your back, you have to wash your stomach yourself.*

- *We get to know one another and develop through exchange and commerce with each other.*

- *To cooperate is to act in pairs.*

In other words, Acte Sept's founding principles are cooperation, respect, independence, graft and resilience. According to Mali's founding fathers, these same principles were supposed to be the moral cornerstones of the nation itself.

Like so many other cultural initiatives, Acte Sept came into being in the wake of the great political and social renaissance that accompanied the overthrow of the military dictatorship and the advent of multi-party democracy in 1991. The hope that energised the nation in those sparkling years is the hope that now lies prostrate, used and abused by a corrupt and self-serving political system. But that hope still smoulders defiantly at the heart of organisations like Acte Sept, who have managed not only to stay alive but also to expand and thrive.

Acte Sept began as a theatre troupe with high ideals not dissimilar to those that motivated Mali's filmmakers. "All people must be able to take part in the cultural life of their choice and exercise their own cultural practices within the limits imposed by a respect for the rights of man and for fundamental freedoms," read their founding statement. The organisation set about implementing these ideals by launching Mali's first international theatre festival in 1994: the *Festival du Théâtre des Réalités.* The festival has taken place in Bamako every two years since its inception. In 2010 it became mobile, visiting cities like Sikasso in southern Mali and others in neighbouring countries.

In 1998, Acte Sept invited a French group called Lo'Jo from Angers in France to come and perform at The Festival in Bamako. The trip was revelatory and included a historic meeting between Lo'Jo and some Touareg from northern Mali who happened to be in Bamako at the time. Through twists and turns, breakthroughs and frustrations, this encounter eventually lead to the creation of the Festival in the Desert, Mali's best-known international music event. The first edition took place in January 2001 in Tin Essako, a tiny sun-baked village about 60 kilometres east of Kidal. Another result of Lo'Jo's trip to Bamako in 1998 was the launch of a new international phase in the long career of Tinariwen, the most famous Touareg band in the world.

Since then Acte Sept has proved to be more than just a theatre company or a Festival organisation. It has helped to nurture writers, actors and theatre technicians. It has fought for the enforcement of copyright law and better distribution of home-grown film and drama; for more stable and better funded cultural organisation; for better links with partners, funders and mentors in Europe; for cultural education and for financial independence in all its activities. Aims such as these would already be a tall order for any European arts organisation, requiring a high degree of intelligence, perseverance, doggedness and courage. In Mali, the challenges and the qualities required to meet them must be amplified tenfold.

In the middle of turbulence that hit Mali in 2012, Acte Sept's inspired founder Adama Traore wrote a new play entitled *Kaklara ou Jamais à Genoux* (*Kaklara or Never on One's Knees*). It was the centrepiece of the 2012 edition of the Festival Théatre des Réalités, which took place in Bamako during November and December 2012. The theme of the Festival was theatre and resistance.

The play revolves around two siblings who symbolise the opposing moral and spiritual currents that have churned Malian society up in recent years. Nièba is a young freedom loving and self-possessed Malian woman who is comfortable both with her femininity and her religion. Her brother Dagaba is a Salafist who is deeply frustrated and embarrassed by his family's 'home-grown' religious observance. He finds their fetish worshipping both intolerable and backward.

Dagaba's mother tries to be charitable and loving towards her intransigent son, although she refuses to wear the black robes and headdress that Dagaba insists a woman must. She also refuses to give up her old gods. "This fetish is the symbol of fertility," she tells him, "I came to it and begged and it enabled me to give birth to you. I accept your intolerance in the name of love, but you only have your version of the truth and no one else's." "There is only one truth," is Dagaba's reply. "You either accept it or you will be eliminated."

"I wrote this piece to show the world that there is resistance taking place here," Adama Traore told a journalist from the British news network ITN in the summer of 2012. "There's been an attack. People have come here with values that aren't the same as ours. We don't share them. They wanted to impose them on us and impose their vision on us. When I heard what was happening in the north, knowing those fundamentalists, I felt I had to do something about it."

Dagaba accuses his sister, wife and mother of being idolatrous *kuffar* or 'unbelievers,' infidels. The strength they draw from household spirits that are allied to a strange sect called Kaklara enrages him. Nièba and her mother try to drug Dagaba, believing this might help him to abandon his strict Salafi beliefs. "This power will detoxify him but you must exercise patience and love," the mother tells Nièba, "because he, like many others of his religion, are like zombies, mutants." Dagaba ends up shooting his sister dead. Adama Traore deserves praise for recognising that resistance requires patience and love as well as courage and persistence.

The programme of the 2012 Festival Théatre des Réalités featured shows by theatre troupes from the four corners of Africa and Europe. It aimed to promote live performance with strong roots in traditional Malian culture. There were over 50 free shows in different neighbourhoods of Bamako and the surrounding area.

One of Acte Sept's main missions is to take theatre to people who rarely if ever get to see it. As well as music, dance, art, film and debate, the Festival offered a theatrical programme focused on themes related to the national emergency. These were some of the programme highlights:

La malice des hommes (*The Malice of Men*) presented by the FLLSL theatre group is about an African dictator who accepts a transition to democracy imposed by the west. He learns how to manipulate a multi-party system to his advantage whilst keeping his Western backers sweet but he meets a tragic end.

Les cinq jours du Mali raconté par Bagnego (*The Five Days of Mali as told by Bagnego*) is a one-man show by the dancer and actor Nouhoum Cissé. In it he retells the modern and tumultuous history of his country, from the first President to the democratic era.

Du gombo pour deux légumes (*Gombo for Two Vegetables*) by Alfred Dogbé was presented by La Troupe Jigiya. The play is all about power, succession and ethnicity in modern day Africa.

Compagnie Kotèbulon's play *Madame Le Maire* (*Madam Mayor*) tells the story of Ramata, a woman whose fight to become mayor of her town puts her in direct conflict with her husband.

The troupe of Ousmane Sow, Mali's most famous modern playwright and director, presented Sow's play *Kalifa et Bandiougou.* Blind Bandiougou and mad Kalifa spend the day shooting the breeze under the Monument to the Martyrs of a fictional Malian town. They talk about the problems of the handicapped, the impoverishment of political life, the revolution of March 26th 1991, and the Islamist invasion in the north and so on. Both men struggle to keep their 'masks' of blindness and madness in place but are eventually revealed to be a pair of crooks and frauds. The play is all about identity, honesty and deception in Mali's political and social life.

As Malian intellectuals are often at pains to point out, theatre didn't arrive in their land with the French *colons.* There was a form of village entertainment, forthright, ribald, amateur and hugely popular, called *Kotéba* or *Nyogolon* that had existed for centuries. Out in the open air, on the village meeting place by the great baobab tree, local men and women would act out dramas of acute local interest: marriage disputes, the custody of children, animal thefts. It was a spontaneous unscripted soap opera in which all the actors, who were always boys or men, never women, and all the storylines were as intimate to the audience as the surrounding lanes and huts.

Kotéba was also riotously funny. In their haste to empathise with Mali's sufferings outsiders often forget to appreciate the comic genius of the Malian people. Laughter is, after all, the cheapest medicine for the fretful soul and Malians know this instinctively. Even the Touareg, with their outward reserve and sombre seriousness, are great lovers of comedy. It is their least appreciated grace.

France brought classical European theatre and layered it over this local tradition, inculcating the students of West Africa's *grands lycées* with a reverence for Moliere, Racine and Shakespeare. The legendary École Normale William Ponty in Senegal, which was responsible for educating most of the politicians and administrators who went on to rule the newly independent states of West Africa in the 1960s, placed a special emphasis on literature and drama. "Intellectuals understood that theatre could be a powerful weapon for mobilisation, organisation and awareness-raising," Malian director Magma Gabriel Konaté told the newspaper *Les Echos*. "The black man needed to define himself by his culture and establish reference points for the emergence of African society."

Before independence, the French Sudan had a small 'native' theatre community, with writers like Seydou Badian Kouyaté and Massa Makan Diabaté pioneering a new school of written Malian theatre. But it wasn't until the National Institute of the Arts (INA) was created after independence in 1960 that this nascent Malian theatre scene began to get support and a little funding. Many of the great Malian actors and playwrights, like Ousmane Sow and Gaoussou Diawara, were nurtured by the Dramatic Arts faculty of the INA in the 1960s and 1970s.

In the 1980s and 1990s, a collective desire to prioritise a truly native Malian style of theatre lead to the creation of the National Theatre in 1979 and National Kotéba Theatre of Mali a few years later. The theatrical establishment slowly turned away from more 'classical' European forms performed in French and towards local forms performed in local languages, especially Bambara. In this new atmosphere, the work of local writers, directors and actors such as Aguibou Dembélé, Habib Dembélé Guimba, Michel Sangaré and Diarrah Sanogo thrived. Kotéba was given pride of place by the new wave.

In response to the increasing putrefaction of political life that occurred in the last years of the military dictatorship, Malian theatre also started to become more politically engaged in the late 1980s. Plays such as *Bougounieri* (1986) or *Wari* (1988) by Ousmane Sow heralded this new radicalism.

Out in the rural villages and communes, traditional Kotéba continued to thrive. Local teachers would often conceive new storylines or even write entire plays for the community, especially when it was felt that the populace needed enlightening about some topic of national importance such as hygiene, transferrable diseases, education, crime, ethnic tolerance and so on. In later years, many public health programmes, including those sponsored by international aid agencies and governmental organisations, were rolled out using traditional theatre. A special company called *Le Groupe Nyogolon*, comprising 20 actors, was formed for this very purpose and it toured the country at the invitation of ministries and NGOs to spread public service messages. More recently, rappers have been fulfilling the same role.

And yet, despite being gorged with talent and promise, Malian theatre still finds it hard to achieve its full potential due to lack of subsidies and institutional support. Alfoune Ifra Ndiaye, artistic director of *La Blonba*, a multi-purpose performance space in the middle of Bamako built and equipped in part with donations from the French city of Angers, which is twinned with Bamako, paints a stark picture of the status quo in an interview he gave to Les Echos: "I'd say that the conditions are far from being ideal for Malian theatre to really exist…I'm talking about regular productions of dramatic texts, regular creation and touring of new plays, the existence of a nation-wide theatre economy, national performance venues, local audiences, critics, cultural activities in schools and directors." The director Magma Gabriel Konaté also told Les Echos that "theatre is the poor relation of artistic production."

Over the past ten years, La Blonba has created 10 new productions that have toured internationally and yielded over 500 individual performances. Alfoune Ifra Ndiaye always tries to work with local actors and has assembled a core team comprising Michel Sangaré, Diarrah Sanogo, Hamadoun Kassogué and the rapper King. Other rappers like Ramsès from Tatapound and Amkoullel have also begun to appear in theatrical productions. La Blonba tries its best to nurture new acting talent.

Ndiaye stresses that a number of different popular performance traditions, apart from Kotéba, continue to nourish modern Malian theatre. "Just as comic Kotéba inspires modern theatre, so do the *ma'ana* or initiation stories, or other folk expression like the masked processions and puppetry etc. One of our creations called *Vérité de soldat* (Soldier Truth) is a ma'ana, a kind of fiction-documentary inspired by the book *Ma Vie de Soldat* (My Life as a Soldier) by Sougalo Samaké. Nonetheless, let's not forget that theatre is essentially a form of expression that came from elsewhere."

Masks are central to the work of the one of the most extraordinary theatre companies to have come into being in the years leading up to the great crisis of 2012. Called Tisrawt, it is remarkable because it was created by local Touareg actors in Kidal, right up in the heartlands of both the Touareg rebellion and the recent Islamist occupation. Tisrawt is the only theatre company that exists in the far north of Mali.

The genesis of Tisrawt is an epic tale in itself. Its origins go back to 2005, when a Parisian theatre company called La

Calma specialising in street theatre and education was invited to Kidal to work with up to 70 local young people and develop their theatrical skills. The first fruit of their work was a programme of short masked sketches that were performed at the Saharan Nights Festival in es-Souk in January 2006. Es-Souk is a ruined city situated about 60 kilometres north of Kidal at the foot of the Tegharghar Mountains where, as I write, the French and Chadian armies are fighting a sustained and brutal battle against the remnants of the Islamist coalition that occupied Mali for ten months from April 2012. Guerrilla warfare aside, es-Souk is a magical place and the sight of so many Kidalian youth, all masked, acting out often hilarious scenarios on subjects as diverse as education, health, pubic hygiene, insecurity and clandestine immigration amplified that magic exponentially. Music for the show was provided by the embryonic Touareg band Tamikrest, then still a year away from launching their international career.

After that inaugural project in 2006, the French actress and director Melissa Wainhouse, a long-standing member of La Calma, returned regularly to Kidal, despite the growing threat of kidnapping and always against the advice of the French foreign ministry. After 2009, the trip could only be made with an escort of bodyguards. She continued to develop short sketches with what had now become a solid core of actors from the Kidal region, both Touareg and Songhoi.

The murder of the British tourist Edwin Dyer by Abou Zeid and his AQIM militia in June of 2009 impregnated the entire northern two thirds of Mali with a heightened sense of danger and paranoia. 2010 was in effect the year that the region shut down to the outside world. Nonetheless, in January 2010, Wainhouse and the players from Tisrawt managed to defy the cowering zeitgeist and perform at the Camel Festival in Tessalit, a beautiful village in the far north east of Mali up by the Algerian border. They also travelled to the Festival in the Desert in Essakane. This was to be Melissa's last visit to the Kidal region before the Islamist occupation of 2012.

Nonetheless, as far as Melissa was concerned, being barred from Tisrawt's home region wasn't reason enough to shelve the whole project. "The only solution was for the actors themselves to come to Bamako," she told me in September 2012. "It isn't an easy task to transport six people from Kidal to Bamako, to house them, feed them and create the right conditions for working." And it wasn't just the logistics that were challenging; it was the novelty of the project itself. "There are no Touareg actors apart from ours and no Touareg theatre troupe apart from Tisrawt," Melissa told me. "But because we were extremely persistent and desirous of success, bit by bit, there was a gathering awareness amongst Touareg leaders and notables of the importance of the work of these young people and what it meant symbolically, even if the troupe wasn't on a professional level yet. It was too early to talk about professionalism but the very fact that these young Kidalois were getting involved and setting themselves the goal of transmitting messages in French and Tamashek through theatre, messages of peace, was important enough in itself."

Whilst the north degenerated into a lawless playground for mafia business and Salafists with AK47s, Tisrawt tackled issues such as trafficking, crime and banditry. At the end of one particular sketch that revolved around these themes, the players would turn to their audience and declare that it was up to them, the Touareg, the northerners, to preserve and value their own culture. It was up to the teenagers and parents of teenagers in the audience to make sure that smuggling and crime didn't destroy society itself. That sketch was performed at the inauguration of the *Biennale Artistique et*

Culturelle in Sikasso in 2010, in front of President Amadou Toumani Touré and a large gathering of dignitaries.

In 2011, Tisrawt received funding from Norwegian Church Aid (AEN) to prepare a new show that would tour the three regions of the north; Timbuktu, Gao and Kidal. A programme of writing, rehearsals and workshops was organised in Bamako, involving professional actors and technicians from La Calma. The ambition was to take Tisrawt to a new level of proficiency and give them the impetus and know-how to carry on developing their art on their own. Nevertheless, with the tumultuous build up to the outbreak of hostilities in northern Mali in January 2012, the tour, which was due to visit schools, cultural centres and festivals in the north, never happened.

The scuppering of Tisrawt's first opportunity to do a well-funded and well-prepared tour was a severe blow. The group had been gearing up to tackling the hardest topic of all; religious extremism. But in the end, with the cancellation of the tour, the opportunity passed. When I spoke to Melissa in September 2012, she was getting ready to go back to Bamako to start a new project with the troupe. Religious extremism was still on top of the list of potential themes for the next phase of work. "Will we tackle the subject of Islamism? Right now I can't say yes or no. It will really depend on the members of the troupe. Luckily theatre allows us to deal with subjects in a symbolic or transposed way, but having said that, the subject is so sensitive. The most important thing for me is not to put them in any danger."

The outbreak of rebellion in January 2012 turned Tisrawt upside down. "In a profound way it was a complete shock," according to Melissa. "Some of the actors took refuge in Bamako and were living a very precarious situation there. Some stayed in Kidal, and were probably caught up in the reality of what was going on. They were sucked into that spiral. I think that right now [ed. September 2012] the youth up there in the north have a very stark choice. If they stay they are forced to ally themselves to one or other of the various movements. Some just don't have the means or the opportunity to leave, because families can't go with them for diverse reasons. You have to realise that this youth wasn't old enough to have been combatants in the rebellion of the 1990s. They were children at the time, but they have been soaked in that whole climate, a climate in which taking up arms has always been a noble act. That is very cultural with the Tamashek. But what's incredible is that I'm in touch with all of them. I've managed to gather my troupe together and all of them tell me that their aim, their only glimmer of hope, is the work of the company."

It was the actors themselves who urged Melissa to let them go and perform in the refugee camps in front of people who have been driven from their homes by the conflict. "Their aim is to make them laugh, to bring them hope and given them a feeling of solidarity and to value their culture, which is in extreme danger right now."

So, in an indistinct fog of crisis and instability, Melissa gathered her players together in Bamako in November 2012 and started work on a new piece called *Tisrawt "Le Royaume d'Idjirane"*. It was about a king who considers himself to be a good king. His motto is "Each man for himself, and everyone for the king." Nonetheless, there's trouble ahead. Drought descends and the harvests are bad. The royal council is convened to try and sort out the crisis. One day a stranger called Albana ('Misfortune' in Tamashek) arrives and announces that a spring called 'Goulou Goulou' is situated right there, under the king's throne. He sows calamity and chaos by pitting one person against the other and manipulating the king. His aim is to make the riches of the kingdom his own. *Tisrawt* was a star attraction at the 2012 Festival des Théatre de Réalités in Bamako.

"Tisrawt is a microcosm of Touareg society," Melissa explains. "That's to say, it is a group of people who come from many different clans. Some are pro-MNLA. Some are pro Ansar ud-Dine. Some are pro-Mali. Others say that it's all nonsense. And the aim is to understand each other, to live together and work together on a common project."

The Tisrawt theatre group is just a beginning, albeit a powerful and promising one. The actors are learning their trade. They're hacking a new trail. "You know, new Touareg bands have it much easier because Tinariwen have already opened up and mapped out the onward path," Melissa said. "They're examples, sentinels, who have reached at least some of their goals. For my actors that doesn't exist yet. They don't have a culture of the theatre. They don't have access to everything that we have access to here in Europe; festivals, books, films. I have to operate at their rhythm. And I'm there, their mother, their sister and their teacher. I'm also their artistic director and I'm determined not to let them become the instrument of another person or entity, nor of the political chaos that the country is in right now."

Heroism is a loud word. It becomes more dignified in its quiet, barely visible incarnations. That quiet heroism exists everywhere, in Mali too, abundant in its obscurity. The quiet courage and dedication of people like Adama Traore, Melissa Wainhouse and the actors in Tisrawt and all the many other small theatre troupes in the country is keeping discourse, culture, education, entertainment and hope alive.

Theatre, in its simplest incarnations at least, costs relatively little. That's why it has power as folk art and as a simple means of bringing problems out into the open where they can be discussed, understood and possibly tackled. In a country like Mali, a country that urgently needs to speak to itself and make its wiser voice heard over the white noise of fear and revenge, theatre is no longer a mere cultural delicacy. It has become essential.

20. Final thoughts

There is a third way

I'm drawing a line under what is in truth an endless subject: it is clear that there's nothing conclusive about the current state affairs in Mali.

As I write, France's Operation Serval is in its seventh week. French and Chadian troops are still battling with Islamist mujahedeen in the Tegharghar Mountains of the far northeast of the country. "We're fighting on the ground at less than a hundred metres from each other," a French army spokesperson told RFI today, March 6th 2013. "The jihadis go from one cave to another and despite their losses, they don't give up."

Abou Zeid and Mokhtar Belmokhtar are reported to have been killed although, in the case of Belmokhtar, verifiable proof of these claims is still scant. Fighters from the Touareg-dominated nationalist movement, the MNLA, are being used as scouts, informers and drivers in the continuing battle. They've also been clashing with Arab smuggling barons at In Khalil, that infamous Saharan mafia entrepôt on the border with Algeria.

Fear and paranoia still suffuses life in the north of the country. Ethnicities that once lived peacefully side by side have been ripped asunder. Arabs and Touareg have been murdered by Malian soldiers or vigilantes or forced to flee their homes. The economy of Timbuktu has been destroyed as Arab shop-keepers and traders have left town. Feelings of vengeance and ethnic hatred remain strong and implacable, stoked by irresponsible journalism and demagoguery. People feel wounded, angry and bitter.

In Gao, the population is still licking its wounds after the ferocious gun-battles that shredded the fragile peace of their town centre in the middle of February 2013. They're also trying to mentally assimilate the brand new phenomenon of suicide bombing, which visited its hateful destruction on Mali for the first time ever on February 8th 2013. That morning, shortly after 6am, an Arab youth with explosives strapped to his body rode up to an army check-post on the northern outskirts of Gao and detonated his load, scattering his limbs in all directions. Thankfully he failed to kill any bystanders.

Suicide bombers – in *Mali*?! Until the end of 2012, the very notion would have been dismissed as fanciful and twisted. Until then, tolerance was one of Mali's steadier sources of pride. The country may have been sinking towards the bottom of all the global indices of poverty, development, education, economic growth and infant mortality. But it was a tolerant place. Everybody knew that. Not long ago, an Arab or a Touareg could leave his camp in the north and travel south to Mopti, Segou or Bamako without fear of personal harm. A Western tourist could book her holiday to Timbuktu, the Dogon Country or even the remote placid Tegharghar Mountains and expect only a warm welcome and a fascinating ride. A local or a foreigner could leave their restaurant in downtown Bamako in the early hours of the morning and walk the streets safely in search of a taxi, or even make their way back to their home on foot. Bamako was infinitely better in that respect than Lagos, Jo'burg or Kinshasa. Suicide bombers happened elsewhere, to other people – in Iraq or Afghanistan. Not in Mali.

Life is different now. The bitterness of the dispossessed has been distilled by conflict into ultimate acts of revenge and self-destruction. 'Lighter-skinned' Arabs and Touareg daren't venture south to the capital, or even to places like Timbuktu and Gao that have been their homes for centuries. Tourism is becoming a distant memory. Democracy and civil society lie in pieces. The future looks uncertain, grim.

The question is, can that fabled tolerance survive all the bile and hatred that ten months of bitter conflict and division have forced up? Can Mali open its doors to the world again and welcome it in?

In many ways, music and culture have been Mali's guardian angels these past few months. Were it not for them, the world would regard the country in the same way as it does the Yemen or Somalia, in other words, as places that are entirely defined by brutality and suffering. Not that Yemen and Somalia don't have their own traditions of music, poetry and art. It is just that the world generally doesn't know much about them. Mali is different.

As has so often been stated by Toumani Diabaté and others, musicians are Mali's true ambassadors, the country's face and voice. Of course the international media has carried interviews with the country's President, Prime Minister and occasionally its Foreign Secretary. But these have been outweighed by the airtime and column inches devoted to the heart-felt reflexions of Salif Keïta, Oumou Sangaré, Fatoumata Diawara, Toumani Diabaté, Cheick Tidiane Seck, Bassekou Kouyaté, Ousmane Ag Mossa or Fadimata 'Disco' Walet Oumar. The silver lining on the cloud of the Malian tragedy has been the limelight that it has afforded Mali's musicians, which has been greater than at any other time in the history of Malian music.

Having a musician rather than a politician speaking for your country has a strangely beneficial effect. A certain enchantment and fascination is mixed in with the usual concern, bewilderment and horror of global opinion. An image that the ordinary man or woman in let's say Britain, France, America or Japan can barely understand or assimilate – such as a young man showing his mutilated handless forearm – is transmitted along with something that everyone can understand, easily and instinctively; music. Human horror and suffering, which disaster-fatigued minds the world over tend to screen out and store away in a place labelled 'the human condition' are balanced with messages of love and hope, with magnetic melodies, bewitching voices and hypnotising rhythms. Music offers a picture of what a proud and peaceful Mali can look like. It gives hope that this state of grace can be achieved again, because it proves that it has existed before.

An attack on music is an attack on the human soul, not just the soul of some distant individual, but on the collective soul of humanity. The world was horrified when it heard that bearded men were amputating limbs in Gao and Timbuktu or stoning young couples to death in Aguel'hoc. But it felt somehow more deeply threatened when it heard that music was being banned in a country whose very name meant little without music and culture. The music ban and the fate of the mausoleums and manuscripts in Timbuktu gave the whole Malian tragedy an angle that seemed to touch our deepest fears. It evoked the universal nightmare of a world without music. It made Mali's crisis seem all the more immediate, urgent and multi-dimensional.

The cynic might say that this only demonstrates the difficulty that we have in empathising with the sufferings of distant fellow human beings. That music or other inanimate cultural objects such as manuscripts sharpen global interest and make empathy easier is perhaps an indictment of our collective heartlessness.

The truth is that our hearts have limited capacity and most of it is invested in the fate of those nearest to us: our families, friends, communities, maybe that of our own nation at a pinch. But music expands the heart's capacity. It can turn a complete stranger into an object of desire, love, respect and veneration. It can make emotional connections across barren distances and frontiers of culture and language. It can create empathy where none would otherwise exist.

If I relate that a man in Gao was arrested and whipped, you might feel horror and disgust.

But if I relate that a man in Gao was arrested and whipped for listening to a tape by Bob Marley or Salif Keïta, aren't your feelings somehow deeper, clearer, more viscerally connected to the actual incident itself?

What's been happening in Mali isn't a war on terror. It is a war on culture; a battle between one view of how the world should be, propagated with the petro-dollars of states and individuals in the Arabian Peninsula and another view that has been nurtured for centuries in the cultural soil of the Sahel, one that mixes the central tenets of Islam with the local cultural colours of West Africa. A similar war is being waged in Pakistan, Afghanistan, Yemen, Tunisia, Egypt and all over the Muslim world. In each territory, this cultural war takes on its own character, with its own specific power plays, strategic imperatives and criminal networks.

Essentially, however, this war imposes the same question everywhere. What is best for society: a rigid and prescribed system of belief and behaviour as laid down centuries ago by the Prophet Mohammed and reinterpreted by scholars such as Mohammed Abd al-Wahab, that bars Western influence of any kind and relies strictly on society's internal resources? Or a looser system of belief and behaviour that allows for local cultural deviation, one that is open to influence from the West and tolerant of outsiders?

In a sense, the choice, as it is often presented, is false. Muslims don't have to choose between pure unadulterated Salafism and Wahabism on the one hand and loose 'Western' corruption on the other.

There is a third way, one that colonialism, post-colonialism and globalisation have unfortunately obscured and in some cases almost obliterated. It requires individuals and governments to trust in their own local culture and traditions; both spiritual and temporal. It requires them to believe that a just system of government, law, education and development can be based on home-grown foundations that are neither Western nor Salafi or Wahabi.

Democracy? Yes, but a democracy that doesn't destroy or cut across old tribal and clan allegiances but incorporates them into a new system of government and state structure.

Shari'a? Perhaps, if the people want it or part of it, but a shari'a that isn't imposed by force and is based on local customs and belief.

Education? Definitely… but education that recognises the importance of local languages and culture.

Development? Of course! But development that is driven by local rather than global needs.

For this third way to be a real option, culture must continue to be vital and strong. This is especially true of music and theatre. They are conduits for the common voice, a voice that desperately needs to be heard as the nation heals its wounds and rebuilds itself.

Music must continue to convey messages of hope and solidarity between the various peoples of Mali, as it has always done. It must build the nation once again as it did in the 1960s. It must continue to represent the country abroad and enchant the world whilst raising awareness about the country's problems. It must continue to entertain, soothe, provoke laughter, draw out sorrow and, in short, make life worth living. As it has always done.

Mali's discredited political class must also wake up to the immense value of their country's music and the beneficial role it must play in restoring peace to their battered land. After all, without music and culture, Mali would merely be an object of pity rather than also one of respect and love.

Andy Morgan
Bristol, February 2013

Read more

For news and information about freedom of musical expression, see www.freemuse.org

For news and information about freedom of artistic expression, see www.artsfreedom.org

APPENDIX – List of Interviewees

Adam Thiam (Journalist)

Afel Bocoum (Musician from Niafunké)

Ahmed Ag Kaedi (Musician, leader of the group Amanar from Kidal)

Amadou Bagayoko (Musician, half of Amadou & Mariam and President of the National Federation of Malian Artists)

Amkoullel (Rapper and founder of 'Jamais Plus Ça!')

Bassekou Kouyaté (Musician)

Cheick Ag Tilia (Musician, member of the group Tamikrest from Kidal)

Cheick Oumar Sissoko (Film director and former Malian Minister of Culture)

Cheick Tidiane Seck (Musician and producer)

Fadimata Walet Oumar, aka 'Disco' (Musician, member of Tartit Ensemble from Goundam)

Ibrahim Ag Ahmed, aka 'Pino' (Musician, member of the group Terakaft from Kidal)

Ibrahim Ag Mohamed, aka 'Massiwa' (Organiser of the Camel Fair in Tessalit)

Lucien Roux (Director of the French Cultural Centre, Bamako)

Manny Ansar (Director of the Festival in the Desert)

Melissa Wainhouse (Theatre Director)

Nina Walet Intallou (Member of the Transitional Council for the State of Azawad)

Ousmane Diarra (Writer and Researcher)

Rhissa (Not his real name. Musician from Kidal).

Rokia Traore (Musician and head of the NGO 'La Passerelle')

Toumani Diabaté (Musician)

Vieux Farka Touré (Musician)

Violet Diallo (Bamako resident and former British Consul)

Yehia (Musician, member of the group Takamba Super 11 from Gao)

www.ingramcontent.com/pod-product-compliance
Ingram Content Group UK Ltd.
Pitfield, Milton Keynes, MK11 3LW, UK
UKHW041946190726
13854UKWH00004B/1826

9 788798 816379